SOPHORA STONE is a spiritual guide, healer, empath, and the visionary behind "Connect for Contact". With over 20 years dedicated to her healing and spiritual journey, Sophora experienced a life-changing extraterrestrial contact that reshaped their understanding of consciousness and humanity's potential. A passionate advocate for discernment and self-discovery, they weave their journey into this transformative work, inviting readers to expand their awareness and embrace a higher paradigm. When not writing, Sophora nurtures their oasis in the desert, finding balance and harmony.

Dedicated to My Beloved Son

You are my constant source of inspiration and strength. Through all
the challenges, you remind me that love, trust, and perseverance make
anything possible. This book is a testament to the journey we have shared
and the boundless potential within us both. May you always know that
with heart and spirit, all things are possible. My love for you is beyond
measure. I love you forever- through every lifetime. - Mama

CONNECT

FOR

CONTACT

My Personal Journey by

SOPHORA STONE

Connect For Contact
My Personal Journey by Sophora Stone
©Sophora Stone

ISBN: 979-8-35098-651-8 (print)
ISBN: 979-8-35098-652-5 (eBook)

TABLE OF CONTENTS

Ground Zero

What is *Ground Zero*? It could have many different meanings to many different people, but they all really mean the same thing. Ground Zero is a significant starting point. It is a moment that has the potential to alter our lives forever. It encompasses various events and experiences that usually leave us with a lasting impact. Things can happen in our lives that change our life and mind in some type of way, such as the tragic events of 9/11 when the planes hit the twin towers in New York City, the assassination of President John F. Kennedy, or even winning the lottery. Circumstances like having a child, the death of a parent, releasing a book, or even making contact with extraterrestrial beings are all Ground Zero events. My life transformed on the night of October 23, 2020. While I did have a belief in inter-dimensional beings or extraterrestrial life, I did not set out that evening with the intention of making contact with them. I was deep in meditation, seeking healing for myself.

My aim for this book is not an attempt to persuade anyone into believing in extraterrestrial life. If you do not already acknowledge their existence, that is your personal journey to explore. Sufficient evidence already exists, and my only hope is for people to question any beliefs that may not be rooted in love. I invite you to join me in a space of acceptance and understanding rather than belief, where acknowledgement replaces the need for faith. By acknowledging the presence of extraterrestrial beings, you can establish a foundation of certainty from which to grow. This foundation of certainty is crucial for initiating contact with extra-terrestrial beings. However, if contact is not your aim, that is perfectly acceptable; personal growth and self-realization do not depend on the belief in extraterrestrial beings. They may appear in various forms, such as ancestral guides, and regardless of how they manifest for you, what matters is how they resonate with you. My experiences with extraterrestrial beings showed up in a particular way to assist me, and they may manifest differently for others. Invoking our ancestors through prayer or ritual is a longstanding tradition in human history, just like extraterrestrial contact. Seeking assistance through prayer and connecting with our ancestors has been a part of human practices since ancient times.

I began my healing journey more than twenty years ago. Although my childhood was filled with a religious theme, my true spiritual journey began later, in 2010, after the passing of my father. I had a profound experience where I encountered his Divine Light after his physical departure. This experience launched me further along the healing path, transitioning it into a journey of spirituality. After that experience, I had no doubt that something greater was waiting outside our physical bodies.

Allow me to introduce myself. The name given to me at my birth is Linda. The name that embodies what I feel today while in a state of connection to my higher self is Sophora Stone, due to various experiences in my life that connected me to the Divine Mother energy and through my strong connection to the land. The name is equivalent to a state of being for me—an energetic frequency I am able to tap into. I identify as a wounded healer or wounded shaman. To be a wounded healer is to transform personal suffering into compassion and helping others on their own healing journeys. It involves embracing one's own vulnerabilities and using them as sources of strength and empathy, helping others navigate their own pain. My deepest desire is to assist in guiding others to become the healers of their own lives. In this book, not only will I share the life lessons I have learned throughout my journey but also share some of what was given to me by the extraterrestrials. My life lessons played a significant role in enabling me to have the contact experience I received, and I hope that by sharing those lessons others will be able to identify what resonates within themselves to help them on their own journey. In essence, this journey leads to inner healing by raising our consciousness to connect with the most loving and authentic parts of ourselves, ultimately guiding us toward our highest self. This is the self that embodies pure unconditional love and is needed to develop our heart's resonance. However, love of this magnitude requires immense courage, strength, and endurance. Unconditional love is far more challenging than one might expect, and it must first originate from within oneself.

Loving oneself completely and without judgment may appear straightforward, but societal conditioning often teaches us the opposite. Many factors can shape our capacity for love and judgment throughout our lives. Childhood experiences, familial relationships, cultural upbringing, and personal traumas all play significant roles in influencing how we perceive love and exercise judgment. As each person embarks on their unique life journey, their capacity for love and understanding will vary depending on their experiences. Unfortunately, my life did not begin under blessed circumstances. I did not receive the experiences of typical young ladies, like dancing classes, Girl Scouts, or parental encouragement to pursue my dreams. In fact, I was not encouraged to envision a bright future at all and, according to my family's beliefs, I had no future. I was raised in a fear-based cult/religious environment that solely focused on the impending Armageddon and the imminent death of everyone that I knew. The only future they described to me was one filled with devastation and destruction. The only glimmer of hope lay in complete obedience, subservience, and conformity to their organization. I was not allowed to have friends outside of the cult/religion, whether they were schoolmates or neighbors. I lived in isolation, cut off from the world that—according to them—had no future. Since no future awaited me, I began to dream of one. I dreamed of the life that I was told would never happen. However, the life that I eventually created exceeded the dreams I had as a child.

How could I dream so big when my future seemed nonexistent during my childhood? I was not supposed to live long enough to drive a car, buy alcohol, or form my own family, let alone experience joy and happiness. I was taught that being happy in this world meant the devil had a grip on your life. Happiness was seen as a sign that you were under temptation, implying that you should be unhappy to prove the devil didn't control you. I was told I could never be happy without their God, without their religious cult, or without them. So, the pursuit of happiness became the driving force in my life. When your family isolates you from the world but forces you to live in it, it makes you feel like an animal in a cage at the zoo, particularly when you do not receive the love you need at home.

I was the fifth and last child, but I was born as the second child to my mother, who had previously undergone a procedure to prevent further pregnancies. Unfortunately, the birth of her third child was a traumatic experience, endangering both her and the baby's life. As a result, her tubes were tied to prevent any future pregnancies. However, a few years later and against all odds, she became pregnant with her fourth child, which turned out to be her first tubal pregnancy. Her religious/cult beliefs were strict on not receiving blood transfusions, and her pregnancy was at high risk because of that and also because it was a tubal pregnancy. Once again, her tubes were tied after this difficult pregnancy. Then, again unexpectedly, three years later, I came into this world as her fifth child, and her second tubal pregnancy. This was a significant time for her because it coincided with the year her religious/cult predicted the end of the world—the end of 1975. Even though my mother believed in this prophecy, fortunately they were wrong and the world did not end. I was born healthy, six weeks before the end of the year. Despite having two miracle children, for a total of five children, this was not the life that she had envisioned for herself. She told me many times that I was not supposed to be here and that she did not want five children. Throughout my entire childhood, I was constantly told that I would forever remain a child, shielded from the worries and temptations of the world, as it was their belief that its existence would come to an end at any moment. The imminent arrival of God was ingrained in my mind, perpetuating the notion that everyone around me could be annihilated at any given moment. When I was a young girl, every opportunity that should have excited me about life was instead thwarted by the devastating messages taught by the cult. I was never offered any positive words, only doomsday prophecies that filled my head.

Being constantly reminded that God will annihilate everyone around you has an incredible impact on the psyche of a child, really anyone, regardless of their age. It made it impossible to plan for my future. When you are told that the future doesn't exist and planning for it is impossible, the blessing arrives when you decide to live fully in each moment. You let go of worries about what's ahead and focus on the present, which becomes a pivotal realization. This is where I actually understood the beautiful lesson behind it all, albeit much later in life. Still, it was a wonderful life lesson and a Ground Zero moment. My traumatic experiences within this religious/cult mirrored those of other religious organizations, mostly pedophilia and corrupt men—and the women who followed their orders blindly. They covered up child abuse within their own hierarchy systems, blaming the children, manipulating them via family isolation, and threatening abandonment. My experiences solidified my belief that such institutions contributed to the broader corruption issues within religions and their structures. Statistics prove that outside of the home, religious institutions are far and away more frequently associated with the highest rates of child abuse. To fully capture my experiences within this religious cult would require an entire book of its own.

However, I will highlight the pivotal Ground Zero moments that profoundly shifted my thinking and undoubtedly impacted my life. Now, I appreciate the significance of each of my experiences in shaping my life as it exists today. Every aspect of my life diverged from the norm, resulting in a manifestation that transcends mere duplication of what already existed around me. I was the *been there, done that* girl. I discerned the flaws from everything I encountered, and endeavored to rectify them within myself, others, and even the world at large. At the time, I was unaware of what I was meant to learn; it wasn't until my awareness broadened that I comprehended the lessons I had learned throughout my life that benefited me and were unique to my own energetic expression of human existence.

I knew there had to be something better out there. I believed in creation, beauty, and love, even though I had yet to find it, probably because I was desperate for it. My mother told me that I was unwelcome back in her home when I left at age seventeen, and she predicted that I would end up as a homeless prostitute on the street simply because I did not want to be a part of the cult. Growing up, I lacked any positive role models. From the very young age of eleven, I was adamant that I didn't want to be like any of them, because all of those I had interactions with were hypocritical. The issue with claiming to be god's chosen people while privately holding the same human tendencies as other churches exposes your flaws once people recognize the truth. Being like the rest of humanity isn't inherently bad; it is the mentality of believing you're superior to everyone else while behaving the same way that makes you appear worse.

I have learned from my experiences that I am capable of healing and moving past any kind of trauma. I have learned to embrace my individuality and how to question authority. I have also learned the importance of empathy and understanding toward others, since everyone has their own struggles and journeys, especially my own mother, who had a childhood full of trauma as well.

Most importantly, I have come out stronger, wiser, and more resilient because of my circumstances. I transitioned from needing to heal from my childhood trauma during my twenties, to embracing the profound lessons imparted in my thirties. Now that I am in my forties, I have integrated all of my lessons and want to share what I have learned, starting off in my golden years. Without all my experiences, I would not have become the person I am today, so I am extremely thankful for my past. The deep reservoir of self-love I possess was attained from those lessons. My mother's role was considerably much more difficult than my own. The unwavering zealot archetype personality has to be quite a heavy burden to bear. When I was able to thank her for everything that happened, I set myself free.

My challenging life, filled with pain and struggle, actually made it simpler for me to discover my inner light. I have been consistently average in life, mostly because I have always needed to exert extra effort to succeed on my own. My determination to succeed stemmed from the necessity to work hard because I was on my own. While I may not have been the master of any particular avenue in life (the result of being alone in this world and spreading my energy across various pursuits), these limitations have granted me a distinctive viewpoint. This perspective allows me to empathize with and identify obstacles that others encounter on their paths. Many people are driven by their egos, attaching worth to specific skills or society's standards, making it a challenge to break free from the constraints of ego-driven perspectives. Coming from humble beginnings has given me a distinct viewpoint after diligently working hard to manifest the life of my dreams. I recognize that true happiness is not found in wealth but in sharing, since I have experienced both scarcity and abundance.

My heart is like a Japanese vase that's been broken a million times but repaired with gold a million times. Now it's almost solid gold because it has been shattered and healed so many times. Every crack and break tells a story of pain and struggle, but also of resilience and strength. The gold represents the love, happiness, and lessons that have filled in the broken pieces, making them even more precious and valuable. My life may have been shattered many times, but I have emerged even stronger and more beautiful than ever before. Like a Japanese vase, I am a masterpiece made even more unique and special because of my imperfections. I have taken every challenging circumstance that life has presented me with and alchemized it into valuable gold, using it as fuel to nourish and enrich the soil of my life, enabling new growth and transformation. I used these lessons in my life to garner strength to change my life early on. Now I use the same concepts to evolve my consciousness and expand my awareness.

The concept of evolution encapsulates humanity's destiny. The moment we realize that we only operate at a tiny fraction of our true capacity can serve as a catalyst for heightened awareness and a longing for something more profound in life. It becomes a moment of reckoning, where we acknowledge our inherent lack of knowledge. Ground Zero represents an opportunity to rebuild oneself to explore new pathways within our minds and unlock our hidden potential. True evolution resides within our DNA; we are constantly searching for ways to unlock it. This process is happening all around us. The moments when we are evolving are characterized by hyper awareness, where answers generate countless new questions. These moments of evolution strip away the comfortable fabric of what we thought we knew, the illusions and comparisons that once defined our lives. Trivial matters fade into insignificance, making room for new experiences and expanded ways of thinking. Sometimes, we must dispose of the old and make space for the newly upgraded manifestations that await us.

Within the pages of this book, I will guide you through a different lens and provide perspectives that inspire deep self-reflection. Whether you are ready for this journey is a question only you can answer. Through introspection, you will explore your own beliefs, examine the inner workings of your mind, and uncover new methods of communication with yourself that you never thought possible. Within you resides immense potential waiting to be unleashed, but it requires dedicated effort to bring it forth. Breaking free from outdated beliefs and embracing a new way of thinking and being are essential. New transformative energies and knowledge are readily available to shape the world we inhabit. If you subscribe to the belief that humans are merely cogs in the system, born only to be charged with a Social Security number and sentenced to a life of work until death with unequal standards of living, then this book may not resonate with you. Perhaps you have never contemplated life on such a profound level before and the shallows of existence are more appealing, providing you with ease and simplicity. Well, that may be perfectly acceptable, and common, but there is a saying that goes "you will never change your life until you step out of your comfort zone."

We find ourselves in the deep end now, where I reside most comfortably. It is here that we must navigate with effort to remain afloat. As a water sign with a filled twelfth house in Scorpio, I am aligned with the vast depths of the ocean. I possess the capacity to hold infinite space, like the cosmos, the ocean, and Mother Earth herself. The ebb and flow of life encapsulates my essence. The deep end, however, resides within my heart, a boundless, ever-expansive space nourished by my growing awareness. Navigating the deep end can be daunting for many individuals. The energy is heavy, and learning to stay afloat requires shedding the weight of heavy baggage, letting go of attachments that weigh us down, and learning to seek help when caught in a storm.

Personally, I have learned how to dance in the perpetual waters, gaining a deep understanding of the grand cycle of our lives. We are meant to learn lessons, grow, and evolve into better humans. To evolve, we must upgrade ourselves, embracing new ways of thinking and acting. While humans retain some animalistic tendencies, our true essence is that of advanced beings, striving to expand our consciousness and reconnect with our authentic self. This quest mandates bravery, for it requires us to face our fears and embrace the possibilities that lay beyond those fears.

Fundamentally, human experiences differ based on energetic imprints at birth and the choices we make throughout life. Nevertheless, we all share common desires, needs, and origins. The human experience is deeply rooted in exploration and expansion; it's not only about retreating into the safety of the caves by the warm embrace of a fire. It is about venturing forth, expanding our horizons, and creating. Our bodies have adapted to this planet over the countless generations we have been here, but our minds must catch up as we have neglected our duty of caring for our Mother and host planet. It is time to recalibrate our connection with the Earth and forge a more unified path of existence.

My journey into self-discovery and understanding my abilities was honed by tapping into the energies of the Earth and connecting with the Divine Mother. During a transformative encounter, Mother Earth showed herself to me through a beautiful purple plant spirit named Sophora Secundiflora. Sophora revealed a mirror to me, where I saw my own reflection. My friends at the time called me Purple Linda. I had purple hair, an entirely purple wardrobe, actually purple everything. Back in 1999, not many people looked like me; I stood out with all my tattoos and vibrant purple locks. I met Sophora in 2000, and we instantly connected. I chose Sophora's name today because she is a medicinal plant and I am a medicine woman. This relationship has flourished within me, filling the void left by the abandonment of my biological mother. The deeper spiritual aspects of this encounter helped me embrace the energy represented by Sophora's name, recognizing the mirror I have become. The presence of red Sophora beans in the possessions of shamans at ancient burial sites suggests that they utilized this plant in some way, possibly as a significant medicinal plant.

That was the Ground Zero moment when I met the Divine Mother energy, and it heightened my awareness instantly. I became conscious of my behaviors and recognized the need to treat her better, understanding the impacts of my actions on her well-being, as well as on my own. I was twenty-four years old when I met her, and I embraced a sense of freedom exploring the world that had been unveiled before me. Growing my own food became a cornerstone of my existence while I nurtured my relationship with the Divine Mother. I dove into my practice and began to learn all that I could about the whole way of thinking and living. During that period, I quickly recognized myself as a magical being, since magic seemed to be constantly present in my surroundings. When I refer to magic, I'm talking about serendipitous synchronicities occurring constantly everywhere around me. I never had to cast any spells to make Mother Earth come alive. Every activity I was engaged in with her ended up with the land, animals, and energy coming alive and engaging back with me. I experienced a connection what felt like that of Snow White, where the plants and animals became my companions. A novice in my practice, I was still young and inexperienced but I knew I was experiencing the influence of karma in my life, constantly showing up in patterns. It would require two decades of dedicated effort for me to comprehensively grasp and integrate these patterns, allowing me to effectively navigate life in accordance with them.

One of the earliest Ground Zero moments I remember in my life was when I began kindergarten at the age of five. A month or so into school, I was beginning to feel more comfortable around the other kids. The Ground Zero moment itself involved a lunchtime conversation with my fellow classmates. As they discussed holiday festivities, I confidently shared the brainwashed jargon the cult had imprinted upon me. I stated that their parents didn't truly love them since they lied to them about figures like Santa Claus, the Tooth Fairy, and the Easter Bunny. I, on the other hand, believed my parents loved me because they told me the truth, which is that they did not exist. Regrettably, I told the other children that they were all destined to die in Armageddon and be forgotten, but without going to hell. Unbeknownst to me, this sparked an uproar, as the children went home and shared with their parents what I had told them, which prompted the parents to contact the school.

I ended up being suspended from kindergarten for a short time. I was forbidden to ever speak a word about the cult's beliefs again. I was shunned by everyone, too. It was at that moment that I realized I was different from everyone else, and the ugly words I had repeated led to widespread hatred toward me. However, as I reached my thirties I understood that this incident was a turning point in my life. At a mere five years old, I learned the valuable lesson about never comparing myself to others. I recognized my uniqueness and embraced it fully, understanding that I did not need to measure myself against anyone else's standards. From that point on, I simply saw myself as a different girl, celebrating my individuality without comparisons. Although I was the unconventional girl, a Goth Emo girl by their standards, I always embraced that identity, so I was comfortable in that role from an early age. That was a beautiful lesson of life, triggered by trauma. Embracing my uniqueness instead of conforming to society's standards was precisely what my life path was meant to entail.

Due to the stark contrast between my upbringing and the experiences of those around me, my dreams strayed far from the norm. Growing up in a fear-based cult, I yearned for the life that was denied to me. I longed for the experiences and joys stolen during my childhood. Visualizing these dreams became my refuge. After I gathered the strength, I broke away from the confines of their cult, leading to their rejection of me in turn. By the time I reached the age of eleven, I had already endured a tremendous amount of trauma. I had outbursts and anger issues stemming from being subjected to the abuse I experienced. I knew I wanted to break free from the people I was forced to be around, as well as the ideologies imposed upon me. Thus, I refused to participate in their activities or attend their meetings. In response, my parents relinquished custody of me to the state, ultimately resulting in my year-long stay in juvenile detention before they found a place for me in a state-run girls home.

Experiencing rejection from one's own family as a tween ranks among the greatest challenges anyone can face in their life. Yet, these deep karmic trenches laid the foundation for the profound gifts that awaited me in the future. Balancing the weight of familial rejection, I developed an unwavering determination to succeed on my own terms, regardless of the circumstances. The theft of my childhood propelled me to cultivate a rich inner world, accessing the visions and insights of my third eye. The absence of familial love fostered within me a heart capable of boundless reception and empathy. These hardships, as heavy as they were, shaped me into the person I am today, preparing me for the challenges and successes that lay ahead. Rejecting the sheep mentality of their cult awakened within me an ability to think strategically, logically, and abundantly. There were no limits imposed on my dreams, no one to tell me I couldn't achieve greatness. Taking a scientific approach to life, I embarked on thorough examinations of various paths and choices. Theorizing came naturally, as I examined the intricacies of each path, contemplating the numerous potential outcomes. Interestingly, during a career astrology report it was revealed that my natural inclination is aligned with the inclinations of a detective, a therapist, or even a writer: each of these vocations resonates profoundly with me. The need to get to the bottom of things—to explore every avenue and examine all possible paths—has become integral to my approach. Critical thinking has become second nature. For those familiar with the Human Design System, my energy type is the Projector—I am called the Seer and Investigative Martyr. Throughout my journey, I have recognized the significance of Ground Zero moments. While these moments may differ from person to person, they share a common thread: life-altering experiences that can serve as a catalyst for change.

My time in the juvenile system and the years I spent in the girls' home during the most influential period of my life could easily fill the pages of an entire book. As I reflect on my time in the girls' home, toward the end of my stay marked a profound Ground Zero moment for me, a lesson that would shape the course of my life. I faced the imminent reality of being discharged from the girls' home at age seventeen without any support, unless I acquired my parents' permission to live at home with them, but to do so I had to succumb to the demands of participating in their cult. I felt trapped and disillusioned. I had the option to not go with them and get kicked out in the few months I had left, or participate in their activities and continue my schooling. My state-appointed therapist pleaded for an alternative path, but those pleas fell on deaf ears as my parents stood firm in their beliefs of "their house, their rules." In those moments, I entered a world of deceit, forced to lie about my true self, my desires, and my own beliefs—the very essence of who I was.

It was a dark and challenging time, one that taught me the corrosive impact of lying and denying my authentic self. Every moment of pretending and concealing my truth felt suffocating, as I yearned for the freedom to be genuine and to live on my own terms. Yet, amidst the struggle, a fire ignited within me: The resolve to never compromise my authenticity again.

Determined to live my truth and break free from the oppressed grasp of their religion, I immersed myself in securing a solid foundation for my future. I studied diligently, balancing vocational cosmetology school, high school, and multiple jobs to attain a cosmetology license and academic qualifications. I was the only teenager I knew who had two jobs while in high school and maintained their own apartment. Remarkably, I emerged triumphant, equipped with a profession and an unwavering resolve to never compromise my true self again.

That Ground Zero moment served as a catalyst for my self-development. It taught me the value of remaining true to my own path, even in the face of adversity. It ignited a relentless pursuit of authenticity and empowered me to build a life where pretense and deception had no place. The lesson I learned from that would serve as a guiding force, propelling me toward a future defined by my truth and unwavering dedication.

Ground Zero moments manifest uniquely for each individual, yet they share inherent similarities, rooted in our human experiences. These experiences shape our lives, but it is our response to these challenges that truly matters. Fear is the pulse of our world, and everyone is fixated on it. That eventually allows fear to control us. Unfortunately, fear-based mindsets lead to the de-evolution of the human conscious, hindering our ability to be present. To expand our consciousness and embrace our true nature, we must summon the courage to face our fears head on.

The mysteries that lay beyond fear are begging us to take brave steps forward, embracing the unknown. In order to master the dance of life within this cosmically charged existence, we must first master our own energetic signatures. Additionally, we can tap into the abundance of elemental energies that permeate our world, harnessing the power to propel our evolution forward. The planets also carry energetic signatures that have served as guiding forces since before humans first began observing and mapping the sky. Ancient cultures from around the globe recognized the significance of celestial movements, each with their own stories and mythologies. Whether Egyptian or Indian traditions, or the myths of the Greeks and the Romans, these stories were gifts connecting us to the source of Divine Energy, offering guidance to humanity. Unfortunately, over time, we have become disconnected from these ancient tools, neglecting the infinite part of our existence that once guided our every endeavor. Instead, capitalism has taken center stage, clouding the true purpose of spirituality and diminishing our connection to our own inner light. When spirituality becomes a luxury reserved for the wealthy, the pursuit of money becomes the substitute for genuine connection and inner growth.

Thanks to this realization, I am on this journey of writing this book, investing in my own website and social platforms, and creating community-based programs. I long to help others find their path to light and abundance, dismantling the barriers imposed by societal divisions, and proving that self-worth is not tied to material wealth. The division of class will be one of the final remnants to dissipate as humanity reaches a higher frequency and potential. Everything you need for spiritual evolution exists within you, available in abundance and free for the taking. It simply requires effort on your part to engage in the transformational process.

Immersed in the enchantment of my magical life, I found magic in everything, even the most trying of times. If anything, the challenging moments offered the greatest transformative power. However, my greatest tool—and one that applies to all individuals—is the power of imagination. Imagination is an energetic signature of the planet Neptune, and since Neptune is the only planet in the first house of my natal chart, it holds a meaningful place in my personality.

Imagination guides our visions, intentions, and personal power. Embracing freethinking, and creating a life aligned with intention and conscious living, proved to be far more fulfilling than conforming to the trends and capitalist ideals propagated on social media platforms. I remained dedicated to following my heart, as my quantum heart became the navigational compass for all of my endeavors. If something resonated with my truth, I spoke it into existence. If someone or something did not align with my values, I stepped aside to remain on the path that resonated with my authentic self. Such dedication stemmed from the signs I consistently encountered along the way. Life presented me with synchronicities and messages, always pointing me in the right direction. To discern the signs, I had to cultivate conscious awareness, which is like attuning myself to the subtle whispers of the universe. Signs are omnipresent in everyone's life. Yet, many individuals fail to acknowledge their presence due to living in an unconscious fashion. They adhere to habits, routines, and ideologies promoted by television, the Internet, and other external influences. By forging a connection with your truest self, rather than relying on the Internet or the opinion of others, you begin to comprehend the damaging impact that it can have on your thought processes, the way that you allocate your time, abundance in all forms, and the overall quality of your life.

Synchronicities often lead to Ground Zero moments. Clearly, I share a profound bond with Stone. It has become my grounding name, inspired by the connections I have forged with the land and my ability to attune myself to the subtle energies permeating my surroundings, particularly within the realm of stone. I often find synchronicities and magical experiences when I am engaging in my most beloved activities, experiencing immense joy. One such activity is rock hounding, which allows me to establish a profound connection through Stone. Throughout my journey, I have stumbled upon numerous incredible ancient fossils and stones. In some of these moments, I have encountered instances where energies are trapped and I am able to release them back into the vastness of space to be recycled.

When distressing events occur, energy can linger within the vicinity of the event's location. This energy becomes absorbed by the surrounding objects and can persist. Since stones naturally carry energy, they have a tendency to pick up and preserve the essence of everything they encounter. This is evident in places that are commonly considered haunted, as they have witnessed unfortunate events and absorbed the lingering energy of them. Furthermore, the significance of stones throughout our recorded history further attests to this notion. We rely on stones extensively for construction purposes to build firm foundations, as well as for crafting jewelry to declare our love for each other. Even in modern technology, stones play the most vital role in components such as satellites, televisions, and telephones because they hold onto energy and information, but can also transmit it.

Remarkably, stones share the same elemental composition as our own bodies, further highlighting their profound connection to us. The desire for immortality drives us to etch our names in stone. We construct monuments that endure the tests of time, ensuring that our legacy preserves, even in the face of societal collapse. Examples like the Rosetta Stone and the Georgia Guide Stones serve as a reminder of this quest to preserve the secrets of survival and a blueprint for societal existence in case of unforeseen circumstances. Through stone, we strive to leave a lasting imprint, transcending the transient nature of human existence.

My ET encounter was not the first mysterious extraterrestrial-related event in my life. Prior to that, I had experienced several other notable moments, all Ground Zero moments that hold significance in my life. As an amateur rock hound, I have explored the ground of every place in the world I have visited. I have also explored various locations across the USA, including the turquoise mines up north in my home state of Nevada. On one particular rock-hounding trip, while driving along a fence that bordered Area 51, we noticed a significant satellite station on top of the mountain. Following directions from my rock-hounding books, we continued on our way. However, as we approached the area, we encountered a narrow road with limited space. Since I was driving a larger SUV, a four-wheel-drive FJ cruiser, it presented little challenge. To our surprise, there was a large pick-up truck stuck in the ditch on the side of the road. The driver, standing outside his vehicle, held up his phone to sky as if struggling to get reception. Interestingly, throughout my rock-hounding trips near Area 51 (and there have been many) I have always had excellent reception, consistently getting five full bars, as compared to my home in the city of Las Vegas, where the signal is considerably weaker with only one or two bars. What caught my attention was the man's license plate, which said AREA 51 in the main area, with VET written down the side in slightly smaller but bold letters, indicating veteran plates, which require credentials to acquire. I felt intrigued, and something about the man seemed oddly familiar. It suddenly struck me—he bore a striking resemblance to a character from the movie *Independence Day*, the scientist working at Area 51. He had long scraggly hair, wore glasses, and exhibited a quirky demeanor.

I couldn't comprehend how his truck ended up in such a precarious position in the ditch. Nevertheless, we did our best to assist, even risking potential damage to my own vehicle; eventually we successfully pulled him out. During the interaction, I felt compelled to explain that our purpose for being there was solely rock hounding. I showed him my books and shared information about the turquoise I had collected, as it seemed obvious that he was curious about our presence in the area. He had a woman in the truck, but she refused to interact with us at all and did not want our attention. I found this very odd considering the situation. Usually people are actively engaged in getting out of their bad situations, but not her.

After successfully freeing the stranded man's truck, we continued on our journey. However, the only available route led us toward the satellite station at the top of the mountain. Sensing an unsettling atmosphere and feeling uneasy about the situation, I proposed that we abandon our plans to explore the rock-hounding spot for the time being and simply leave. It was evident to me that the character in the movie was inspired by this man we encountered. The resemblance was striking, leaving no room for doubt in my mind. Despite my curiosity, I hesitated to ask any probing questions or appear overly intrusive. I respected that it was not my place to pry into his affairs or be nosy, given the circumstances. At the top, the station had many no-trespassing and keep-out signs, and there were cameras set up to monitor the site. We gladly turned around and headed back down the mountain the same way we came.

The most peculiar aspect of the encounter was the woman who remained in the passenger seat of his truck the entire time. Curiosity compelled me to sneak a glance at her, but she appeared to deliberately avoid meeting my gaze. I found this behavior strange, especially considering the fact that we had just rendered assistance by pulling them out of a ditch on the side of a mountain. The encounter was lengthy, but she did not want to engage with us in any way, so much as to not look me in the eye or even say thank you. Although there was no direct encounter with a UFO or extra-terrestrial being, the experience of meeting and assisting the person who undoubtedly holds an extensive amount of knowledge on the subject is profoundly significant to me—a Ground Zero moment I will always cherish.

Prior to living in the desert of Las Vegas, I used to reside in Colorado. One evening I was beckoned outside to observe a perplexing and erratic light in the sky. It moved in an unconventional manner, unlike any aircraft, star, or celestial phenomenon we had ever encountered before. The light appeared to sway back and forth, ascending and descending, albeit at a slow pace. Captivated by this inexplicable sight, I dedicated several hours to observing the craft's actions, and it became evident that it was indeed a sophisticated craft that was engaged in some kind of activity. Even this simple event holds immense significance in my life, and similar events can do the same for anyone who witnesses something like this. Witnessing a star-like object in the sky, moving in an unconventional pattern, triggers our minds to explore the countless possibilities that it could be. This glimpse of the extraordinary can be a Ground Zero moment for those who have never encountered anything beyond the ordinary. It creates pathways for personal evolution, expanding our perception of what is possible in life.

That's why each one of these documented sightings is important. This is the typical UFO phenomena that people usually witness and are captured on film. The typical camera film footage of UFOs often captures intriguing and erratic visuals. These films showcase unidentified flying objects in the sky that are exhibiting peculiar flight patterns, extraordinary speeds, and unconventional maneuvers. Such footage aims to document and provide evidence of these unexplained aerial phenomenon, stimulating curiosity and further investigation into the mysteries surrounding UFOs. The general public is wildly familiar with this category of aerial phenomena, and the evidence upon which most people base their beliefs. Even governments have now publicly acknowledged the authenticity of these aerial phenomena, confirming that the lingering conspiracy theories were indeed grounded in truth.

One thing is certain—millions of people have witnessed and documented these aerial phenomena for centuries (in fact, for much longer). I am confident acknowledging that they have always been here because of the evidence they have left behind, as well as my knowledge on the subject after my experience; now we simply have better ways to share our information than ever before. In this extraordinary era of heightened curiosity, it becomes crucial for us to comprehend the reasons behind these unexplained occurrences and the intentions of the extraterrestrial beings involved. If the subject intrigues you, I aim to shed some light on it.

To determine if this path aligns with your interests, consider reflecting upon a few questions, found below. Explore the origins of your own perspectives and beliefs, evaluate where you are currently directing energy in your life, and discern how open you are to exploring new possibilities. Ultimately, the decision of whether or not to embark on this exploration rests solely within you, as it requires a personal understanding of your own background, belief system, and the focal points of your life.

These thought-provoking questions can help you reflect on your current state of awareness, gain insight into your desires, and begin an inward journey of self-discovery and personal growth. Meditation is a key, and you are the keyhole to the door of the life of your dreams. Your old keys will not unlock any new doors for you.

- What truly brings me joy and fulfillment in life?
- Am I living in alignment with my values and authentic self?

- What fears or limiting beliefs are holding me back from pursuing my dreams?

- How do I define success, and am I working toward achieving my own definition of it?

- What emotions or patterns do I need to heal or release in order to experience inner peace?

- Am I nurturing my physical, mental, and emotional well-being?

- What contributions do I want to make to the world, and how can I start taking action toward that?

- Are my relationships nourishing and supportive, or do I need to make changes?

- What role does gratitude play in my life, and how can I cultivate more of it in my life?

- Am I being true to myself and living authentically, or am I conforming to societal or familial expectations?

CONNECT
FOR
CONTACT

CHAPTER 1:
Where to Begin—Deciding if This Path Is Right for You

As you embark on your journey, it is highly likely that you are already on the path of self-actualization. Regardless of your current position, whether you feel drawn toward something or are simply curious about contact experiences, you must first understand what this path entails. Throughout this book, my aim is to provide insight and guidance for individuals at various stages on their journeys. Whether you are just beginning or consider yourself advanced, I hope to meet you where you are and support you in making the most of this book during your journey on this path. The essence of this book is discovering oneself, which involves embracing self-acceptance as the initial step toward self-improvement. The foundation of self-love on our path is immensely crucial.

So, what is the path? This is the path toward evolution of consciousness. The path is about connecting with your true self. It is a journey that leads you toward unconditional love, starting with loving yourself. It is the path to your inner light, to happiness, and to the interconnectedness of all things. This is your infinite conscious self. Consciousness is our source of creation, which is love – the divine energy – and is at the core of how we came into existence. A lifetime on this planet is a gift, with all the emotions, the messiness, and the lessons serving as means for growth. Reincarnation offers us the opportunity for our souls to evolve and propagate our species on as many planets as possible, leading to the creation of diverse versions of ourselves, making us all interconnected as brothers and sisters. Advanced consciousness technology surpasses the comprehension of human minds in their current state of development, and there are control mechanisms in place for us that indicate that our minds are not ready to appreciate such concepts. Understanding that our evolution on this planet is intricately linked to our DNA, thanks to their surveillance, we can perceive their affection for us, even if our existence is technically an ongoing scientific experiment. Everything was made from their love of their own and sustained by love; love from a species that took control of their own evolution a very long time ago. They created everything for us and brought us here to flourish and expand from their genetic material, also known as their DNA. They have created a light consciousness system so that our species gets to live again and again, evolving our hybrid bodies. We can see this when we look out into space; there are an infinite number of spiral galaxies, each holding the potential for diverse life forms on their own evolutionary journeys, and it's our playground.

When I speak of light, I am referring to it as a means of transporting our soul. Light serves as the vehicle for our soul during transitional phases, from one physical form to another. While our souls' essence may manifest as light—such as the light at the end of the tunnel in near-death experiences, or in the stories of Divine Light like Jesus aka Yeshua, or Buddha—it primarily acts as a mode of soul transportation. Light is not our permanent state but a way for our soul to navigate diverse experiences in the universe.

Understanding these concepts can be too complex for our human brains to comprehend. We have been imprinted upon, programmed, and conditioned to be judgmental, both of ourselves and of others. Society has fostered divisions based on factors such as race, class, and sex. Conditional love has become the norm, love that comes with strings attached. If they made everything with love but we fail to see ourselves in everything, then do we know or understand love?

While we have experienced certain forms of conditional love, that is not the kind of love that I am referring to. To find this place of true love, we must confront and release the conditioned beliefs that have been ingrained in us. We must detach ourselves from these conditions and examine whether they stem from a place of genuine love or if they are merely societal influences intended to promote separation.

Many individuals have placed their trust in various governing political systems, as it is designed to govern the people. However, the past century has highlighted the broken nature of the system. Those in positions of power often prioritize corporate interests over the well-being of ordinary citizens, focusing on profit margins rather than sustainable progress. Witnessing the destruction of our host planet without taking proactive steps toward sustainable practices reveals a concerning disregard for Mother Earth's well-being. Relying on and investing love into a flawed system is just like a confined hamster on its wheel—perpetually running yet getting nowhere.

The global shift in consciousness triggered during the time of the pandemic prompted people to awaken to the reality of this system's operations. For those who have been aware of these issues, witnessing increased awareness amongst others is heartening, signaling the potential for a transformative New Earth. To progress, we must cultivate faith in ourselves rather than in the flawed system that has led us to this point. A crucial element for this growth is forgiveness. Assigning blame is unnecessary. Every event has culminated in this present moment, providing us with the necessary ability to recognize the shortcomings of this unbalanced system and to instigate change. Human creations inherently contain flaws due to our limited understanding and capabilities. Similar to ascending a ladder, every rung plays a vital role; each step supports our progression to the next level. The significance of the initial step mirrors that of the middle and final steps—each one is imperative. Without the foundational first step, reaching the ultimate final step would be unattainable. When we relinquish blame and embrace accountability, this marks the origin story of our journey. At this juncture, you must decide if this path is right for you. Are you willing to dive deeply into yourself? Are you willing to look at the workings of this world in order to be a part of the change for the betterment of every single person on this planet? Do you want to know your true self? Do you desire unconditional love for yourself and for others? Are you ready to illuminate the path that leads to love, the path to finding the Divine Light source within you?

Breaking down the fabric of your reality becomes imperative, in order to illuminate the way toward the source of Divine Love energy. This path is spiritual in nature, but it does not lead to any particular religion. It is a personal relationship with the conscious light energy system of our creator beings—the source of all that exists for us as we are in this human form. When you connect with true love, you will find peace within your heart. There is no room for judgment; instead, compassion for all beings becomes your guiding principle. You will be able to meet others where they are on their own journeys, without comparing yourself to them. Judgments and comparisons with others have no place on this path. Those are shadows that cloud our ability to see love in its true form. The only judgments should be of your self and your own progress, or of adhering to your boundaries.

To truly understand the path, we must examine the societal judgments, comparisons, and competitive nature that provide our existence. Although significant strides have been made in combating racial segregation in the past hundred years, we still grapple with it, as well as gender inequality and, more prominently, the separation of classes. The question arises: How can we truly treat everyone equally and embrace love equally? Given that this is an individual journey toward self-discovery, it is essential to examine ourselves without comparing ourselves to others. Each person's story and experiences will differ, shaped by their own unique perspectives, beliefs, and behaviors. Every human experience possesses its own distinct energetic signature, dancing its way through the cosmos. This is where meditation proves invaluable. Meditation allows us to quiet the mind, regulate our breathing, and relax, preparing us to be fully present in the current moment.

Humanity cannot evolve without the presence of children. Choosing to become a parent in today's world is a courageous and noble act. Engaging in self-work and imparting those lessons to your child has the potential to transform our future. Many have forgone the opportunity to bring life into this world. Feminine energy is amplifier energy. When you provide a woman with sperm, she will give you a child; if you give a woman a house, she transforms it into a home for you both. If you buy a woman provisions, more than likely she will cook you a meal. If you challenge a woman, undoubtedly she will respond with greater intensity. Just as planting a seed in Mother Earth yields food, tending to her land ensures she will sustain you for a lifetime. A woman's womb is a sacred vessel, a gateway where souls journey into this realm. It is essential for awakened parents to instill in their children the teachings that surpass what they themselves received. By dedicating even just one generation to imparting different values to our children, everything can be changed. A woman has the power to alter humanity's paradigm by raising even a single child.

Some people possess an unwavering feeling that they're destined for more, or they long for something better. They strive to become better people, or better parents, every day. They face setbacks with resilience. They are on the path of change and evolution of consciousness, but they may not have known what this path entails or how to navigate it. The next step on the journey may seem daunting, especially when it differs from the conventional beliefs or understandings of many. The life of a conscious adult and conscious parent varies greatly depending on our individual realizations in the present moment, our spiritual self-discovery, and the energetic signatures of the astrological imprint at our birth. These factors contribute to our current state of awareness. It would be small minded to assume that all experiences or perspectives should be the same or even similar, considering the vast diversity of human existence—eight billion unique journeys—each with their own merit—on this planet alone. To those disinterested in parenthood, whether they think it might be too difficult for them or for the child because of the conditions of the world, I urge you to consider where true growth unfolds. It is mirrored in all aspects of life; it is the universal law of "as above, so below." When new land arises from the sea, it's due to a shift in the tectonic plates and the eruption of a volcano, leading to the creation of new terrain from the pressure and ensuing lava flow. In a similar manner, I emerged from the pressures of my upbringing and cultivated a better life. Not everyone can achieve this, which is why we need everyone to be actively engaged. Adversity tends to breed exceptional individuals. Each of us is a diamond emerging from the rough, the pressures of the conditions around us.

For those who may not be interested in the path to true self-connection for contact experiences, you may choose to skip ahead to read about my own personal experience. The following chapters will focus on the belief that everyone has the capacity to make contact experiences real, even though not everyone may achieve it. Typically, for those who believe they can find their light or establish contact, it is within reach. Those who are confident in their abilities will succeed. Those who doubt that it is possible for others or themselves never will. This book provides a self-evaluation process, eventually guiding you to connect with inter-dimensional beings through your higher self (if this is what you wish to work on), as that is the realm where they can communicate with us.

Contact with them only serves the purpose for our growth and evolution. That is their mission. Engaging with them transcends superficial or insignificant issues lacking in evolutionary value. Their contact is rooted in assessing where assistance is genuinely needed and determining their ability to provide it. Desiring contact does not guarantee it will manifest. As humanity collectively gains awareness of the circumstances, our capacity for contact will increase. However, prevalent adherence to outdated belief systems leads many to disregard obvious evidence already in existence. They are here for us, because we are a part of them.

For those who feel an unwavering pull toward self-exploration and personal development—a yearning for something greater—this path offers a space for growth and transformation. It is a constant process of becoming more aligned with our true selves. Setbacks are met with resilience and are seen as opportunities for growth. The journey can be challenging, and may involve confronting beliefs and facing uncomfortable or even ugly truths, but it is through these experiences that we expand our consciousness and find the inner strength necessary to navigate the path. The prospect of embarking on a journey that challenges societal norms and expands our understanding beyond what we have been taught can be scary. However, for those who desire to awaken to their true potential, possibly connect with inter-dimensional beings, and expand their conscious awareness, this path offers the tools and guidance needed to embark on that sincere self-evaluation.

As we progress on this path, it is crucial to approach our experiences with a sense of curiosity and open-mindedness. Everyone's journey unfolds uniquely, shaped by their own spiritual understanding and life path; humans have had close to 10,000 religions on this planet. While some may be guided by a deep conviction, others may be driven by a sense of curiosity or the search for higher truths. Regardless of where you begin, it is essential to release the need for comparison and judgment. Each path is valid, and no two journeys are the same. By cultivating self-awareness and avoiding the trap of comparing ourselves to others, we can honor the authenticity of our individual experiences.

One integral practice that supports us on this path is meditation. Meditation serves as a powerful tool for quieting the mind, centering ourselves, and cultivating present-moment awareness. In the stillness of meditation, we create space to connect with our true essence, accessing the wisdom that resides within us. Through regular meditation practice, we can develop a deeper understanding of ourselves, untangle our conditioned patterns of thinking, and establish a stronger connection with our higher selves. Meditation is free. Movement is free.

Yoga is also a free tool that follows a comparable trajectory—connecting with our inner light and nurturing love for all beings. The Yoga taught in western society primarily emphasizes physical exercise benefits, overlooking the dance it engages with the universe and divine energy. It is important to remember that this path does not lead to a specific religion or belief system. It is a personal journey toward self-discovery and a quest for connection to our true selves, as well as connection to the energy that permeates all of existence. By cultivating a one-on-one relationship with ourselves, aligned with forgiveness and love, we align ourselves with the source of all creation.

On this path, we discover deep peace within our hearts, transcending judgments and comparisons. Love becomes our guiding principle, encompassing all beings and fostering a sense of compassion and unity. As we navigate the path, we encounter challenges, mishaps, and moments of doubt. We may question whether the path is for us and whether we can truly attain the level of self-connection or self-love necessary to achieve the contact experiences that we seek. It is in these moments that we must remind ourselves of our inherent worthiness and capacity for growing. The path is not linear, and it's normal to experience moments of uncertainty and resistance. It's through embracing these problems with courage and perseverance that we can truly awaken to our fullest potential and explore the depths of our consciousness.

It is my hope that this book serves as a guiding light on your journey, providing insight, inspiration, and practical tools to aid you in connecting with your true self, and ultimately getting to experience contact with our Creator beings and inter-dimensional guides. Each chapter offers an opportunity for self-reflection and introspection, inviting you to dive deeply into your own consciousness and answer the questions about your own conscious awareness. There are no wrong answers, as these are only navigational questions to help you understand where you are and help you get to where you want to be. Remember, this journey is unique to you, and no matter where you are on your own voyage, you're exactly where you need to be. Embrace the unfolding of your own transformation and trust in the wisdom and guidance that will emerge as you embark on the path of self-discovery and connection.

Although I would say it has been a lifelong spiritual journey, I began my true spiritual healing journey at the age of twenty-four when I met the Divine Mother. I made contact at the age of forty-four, signifying a twenty-year process to harmonize the knowledge gained from my healing and spiritual path, which culminated in extraterrestrial contact. The organic nature of my journey likely contributed to its duration. The path forward was never clearly defined, and I encountered numerous challenges that served as important lessons. I had not foreseen that the journey would lead to this point of contact with extraterrestrials. Now, I truly want to help accelerate humanity's contact experiences and prompt a more rapid paradigm shift for us all.

Extraterrestrial experiences, or encounters with inter-dimensional beings or phenomenon beyond Earth have long fascinated and captivated the human imagination. These encounters ignite a sense of curiosity and wonder, prompting individuals to explore the possibility of life beyond our planet. Most extraterrestrial experiences that are depicted in movies and pop culture are usually negative or threatening in some way, but actual human encounters are positive, spiritually enlightening, and transformative in nature. These experiences provide a glimpse into the broader cosmic reality and hold the potential to expand our understanding of the universe and our place within it.

Positive extraterrestrial encounters take various forms, each offering unique insights. One type of encounter involves people reporting contact with benevolent beings who convey messages of love, unity, and spiritual evolution. These encounters often involve a heightened state of consciousness, telepathic communication, and a profound sense of peace. Messages from these encounters often emphasize the importance of love, compassion, and the awakening of human potential. Another type of positive extraterrestrial experience involves individuals recounting interactions with these advanced civilizations or beings from other realms and dimensions. These encounters may occur during deep meditative states, or through astral projection, lucid dreaming, or out-of-body experiences. These experiences often provide insight into the nature of consciousness and the interconnectedness of all things, as well as the vastness of the universe. Individuals may receive profound teachings, spiritual guidance, or glimpses into higher dimensions of existence. Spiritually enlightening extraterrestrial experiences often reveal a deeper understanding of the nature of existence and provide a catalyst for personal development and transformation. They open people up to new perspectives, challenge belief systems, and invite a deeper exploration of consciousness and the mysteries of the universe.

People are drawn to these experiences because they offer a sense of meaning, purpose, and connection. Those drawn to exploring extraterrestrial encounters may seek a variety of benefits from their exploration. One benefit is the expansion of perspective and worldview. Extraterrestrial experiences challenge our limited understanding of reality and present the possibility of consciousness existing beyond our physical forms. Exploration of extraterrestrial encounters can foster personal and spiritual growth. These encounters catalyze profound shifts in consciousness, prompting people to question deeply held beliefs and embark on journeys of self-discovery and self-exploration. The quest to understand and integrate these experiences often leads to an expansion of awareness, increased intuition, psychic abilities, and a renewed sense of purpose. Extraterrestrial experiences can offer a sense of hope and inspiration. They remind us that we are not alone in the universe and that there is a grand tapestry of life waiting to be explored. These encounters challenge the limits of what we perceive as possible, reminding us that our existence extends beyond the confines of Earth. The search for meaning and purpose takes on a whole new dimension as we contemplate our place within the vast cosmic story unfolding around us.

It is important to approach the topic of extraterrestrial experiences with an open mind and discernment. While there are numerous accounts of positive and spiritually enlightening encounters, it is crucial to critically evaluate and discern the authenticity of individual experiences. Discernment can help separate genuine encounters from fabricated stories, usually made up for profit such as Internet likes or views, or are simply a misinterpretation of mundane phenomenon. The exploration of positive and spiritually enlightening extraterrestrial experiences offers a glimpse into a broader cosmic reality and invites us to consider profound questions about our place in the universe. People are drawn to this topic, seeking an expansion of their perspective, human development, and a renewed sense of purpose. By exploring these experiences with an open mind, individuals can embark on a metamorphic journey and end up with a deeper understanding of their place within the vast cosmic tapestry.

Embarking on the exploration of extraterrestrial encounters is extremely thought provoking and requires emotional and psychological preparation. Before diving into the topic, it is crucial to engage in self-reflection and to honestly assess your motivations, fears, and beliefs. This introspective process allows people to gain a deeper understanding of their readiness to confront the mysteries and possibilities that lie beyond our earthly realm. Honesty with yourself is essential to reflecting on the motivations driving your interest in extraterrestrial encounters. Ask yourself questions like, Am I genuinely curious about expanding my understanding of the universe? Am I seeking validation or a sense of belonging? Am I approaching this exploration with an open mind, or being influenced by preconceived notions?

Being honest about our intentions helps us discern whether we are sincerely prepared for the challenges and revelations that may come with this journey. Exploring the topic of extraterrestrial encounters can invoke a range of emotions and fears. It is important to identify and understand these emotions and fears, as they may influence our perceptions and reactions. They can even influence the contact experience itself or inhibit if all together. Are we driven by excitement, curiosity, or a sense of adventure? Do we feel apprehension, fear, or skepticism? Our fears and emotions, if not managed correctly, can hinder our progress by creating resistance to our alignment with desired outcomes. Emotions and fears often influence our actions more significantly than we realize, increasing resistance to our manifestations. Attaining greater control over our focus is key to overcoming the resistance. In stillness, we can cease to resist. Acknowledging our emotions and fears allows us to approach the exploration with greater self-awareness, ensuring that we navigate the journey in a way that aligns with our emotional and psychological well-being.

Beliefs play a significant role in how we interpret and process information. When it comes to the topic of extraterrestrial encounters, our beliefs may be shaped by cultural, religious, or society's conditioning. Are we open to challenging our existing beliefs and expanding our worldview? Are we willing to consider alternative perspectives and entertain possibilities that may contradict our current understanding? Exploring these questions helps us examine the foundation of our beliefs and assess our readiness to explore this topic from a place of openness. To aid in the self-reflection process, here are some prompts to consider.

- What initially sparked my interest in extraterrestrial encounters? How do I feel when I think about exploring this topic?

- What are my motivations for delving into the subject? Am I seeking validation, excitement, a sense of belonging, or genuine knowledge?

- What fears or concerns do I have about exploring extraterrestrial encounters? What might be driving those fears? Are they based on personal experiences, societal conditioning, or misinformation?

- How open am I to challenging my existing beliefs about the nature of reality, consciousness, and the possibility of life beyond earth? Am I willing to consider alternative perspectives and entertain the unknown?

- What are my expectations for this exploration? What do I hope to gain or discover by engaging with the subject of extraterrestrial encounters? How do these expectations align with my personal growth and development?

- Am I emotionally and psychologically prepared to confront the unknown and the potential paradigm shift that exploration of this topic might bring? How will I navigate any unexpected challenges and revelations?

"Cheers to all the people who can change their minds when presented with information that contradicts their current beliefs"
—Unknown author.

This meme caught my attention on social media because it is a reminder to stay open to accept change, preparing for growth at any time. Engaging in the self-reflective process allows us to establish a strong foundation for exploring this topic. It encourages an honest assessment of our motivations, fears, and beliefs, leading to a more aligned and fulfilling journey of exploration of this topic. Self-reflection is a valuable tool that supports our personal development, introspection, and open-mindedness—all essential components for those prepared to venture into the mysterious realms of the cosmos and contemplate the possibilities beyond our planet.

Exploring the topic of extraterrestrial encounters comes with inherent risks and challenges. It is important to acknowledge the potential risks and be prepared to navigate them effectively. Some of the risks involved include skepticism from others, feelings of isolation, or being misunderstood, as well as the potential for frightening experiences. However, with conscious awareness and thoughtful strategies, these risks can be mitigated, ensuring a more fulfilling and safe exploration.

One risk that individuals may encounter when exploring this topic is skepticism from others. Our individual beliefs and experiences differ, and not everyone shares the same interests or open-mindedness. It is crucial to remember that each person's perspective is valid, even if it differs from our own. If someone holds steadfastly to their own specific beliefs and cannot accept that you have your own, it is essential to exercise discernment over judgment. You should consider whether you desire or require the presence of such an individual in your life. If you can accept someone for who they are but they cannot reciprocate that acceptance for you, it is often best to walk away. Otherwise, you risk being influenced by their energy.

To mitigate this risk, it can be helpful to seek out like-minded communities and individuals who share the same interests on the subject. Engaging in discussions, joining online forums or social media groups, or attending conferences and events focused on extraterrestrial encounters can provide a supportive network of individuals who understand our feelings of isolation or being misunderstood. It is natural to seek connection and understanding from others. Surrounding ourselves with people who are open minded and accepting of our interests can offer peace, thereby fostering a sense of belonging and reducing feelings of isolation. Developing meaningful connections within these communities can provide a safe space for sharing experiences, engaging in discussions, and finding support.

Another risk related to exploring this topic is the potential for having negative or frightening experiences. If your mentality is rooted in fear, then fear is what you will attract in life. The energetic frequency you align with mentally determines what you will receive. This is why it is essential to do the preparation work. We need to approach the subject with discernment and caution. Keep in mind that not all reported encounters or information may be reliable or accurate. To mitigate the risk, it is advisable to research credible sources, critically evaluate the information, and approach personal experiences with a levelheaded mindset. Trusting our intuition and our inner guidance can help us navigate potentially challenging or unsettling experiences, ensuring our emotional and psychological well-being. If at any point during exploration, your feelings of distress, fear, or confusion become overwhelming, seeking professional help from qualified therapists, counselors, or support groups may be helpful. These professionals can provide guidance, offer resources, and help navigate any psychological or emotional difficulties that may arise.

It is important to note that discussing topics related to extraterrestrial encounters often falls within the realm of personal beliefs and experiences. As with any subject matter, it is essential to approach the topic respectfully. It is important to emphasize that engaging in the exploration of extraterrestrial encounters carries personal responsibility. Individuals are encouraged to exercise their own discernment, conduct thorough research independently, and consider the potential risks associated with seller involvement; referring to any people, groups, or organizations that market specifically to the ET community. The responsibility for personal choices and interpretations remain with the individual exploring the subject matter.

Examining our beliefs about extraterrestrial life and the possibility of contact is a crucial step in our personal exploration. Our beliefs shape our perceptions and interpretations of the world around us, influencing how we understand and interact with the concept of extraterrestrial life. It is important to recognize the different belief systems that may influence our experiences and how we navigate potential conflicts that arise with varying perspectives. When exploring the possibility of extraterrestrial contact, our existing beliefs do impact our interpretation of the experiences. Those who hold strong beliefs about the existence of extraterrestrial civilizations may be more open and receptive to encounters, interpreting them as confirmation of their beliefs. On the other hand, individuals who hold skeptical or dismissive beliefs may be more inclined to explain such encounters as mundane phenomena or misinterpretations. It is crucial to approach this exploration with an open mind, allowing space for new information and possibilities to emerge.

In the current landscape, it is more vital than ever to engage in these meaningful efforts, especially in light of the rapid emergence of new technologies. Innovations like AI and holographic technology have the potential to create misleading images and videos. Navigating conflicts between different belief systems and new technologies requires knowledge, empathy, understanding, and open communication. It is important to approach discussions with respect for different perspectives, as well as willingness to listen to and learn from others. Seeking to find common ground in areas of connection helps facilitate a healthy exchange of ideas and experiences. Remember that beliefs are deeply personal, and can be rooted in diverse cultural, religious, and philosophical frameworks. Embracing a spirit of curiosity and humility allows for growth and promotes a deeper understanding of the complexities surrounding this topic.

Throughout this journey of exploration, self-reflection and preparation are paramount. Taking the time to examine our own beliefs, biases, and preconceptions allows us to approach the topic with greater clarity and discernment. Reflection helps us understand how our beliefs may influence our perceptions and interpretations of experiences. They can reveal areas where our beliefs may limit our ability to embrace new ideas and concepts. Engaging in self-reflection also helps us cultivate the emotional resilience and patience needed to navigate potential challenges or conflicting information that may arise through new technologies.

It is important to be patient with ourselves, and the Internet, as we explore this expansive topic. The path to understanding extraterrestrial life and contact can be one of continuous growth and evolution. Our beliefs may transform and adapt as we gain new insights and experiences. It is essential to give ourselves permission to evolve and to reassess our beliefs in light of new information and perspectives. Investigating and seeking the true origin of any Internet content regarding extraterrestrials is crucial for discerning fact from fiction. By delving into the authenticity of such contact, we can separate potentially misleading or fabricated material from genuine evidence, contributing to a more informed and rational discourse regarding extraterrestrial phenomenon. This process not only supports the pursuit of truth, but also fosters critical thinking and responsible evaluation of extraordinary claims in this digital age.

Seeking out resources and support is a valuable aspect on this journey. I prefer free-contact groups, because I understand that extraterrestrials do not use money and are not interested in it; money is irrelevant to them. When a group's access is determined by financial status, it hinders the real purpose of making contact. While some may profit from this, true contact should not be limited by affordability. Engaging with reputable books, documentaries, and research papers can provide a foundation of knowledge and different perspectives to aid in your exploration. Joining free support groups, attending free conferences, or participating in free online communities can offer a sense of belonging and provide opportunities for open discussions and the sharing of experiences. I discuss the concept of free groups because our existing flawed capitalist system continues its cycle of dysfunction if this is the sole ambition that society pursues. If aspiring to be an entrepreneur in a capitalist society is considered the ultimate goal, are we not inevitably bound to prioritize money and the commercialization of goods, services, and even spirituality?

We should also be aware of those who only believe in their own experiences and dismiss others'. There are free resources and support systems that can help validate our experiences and provide guidance when faced with uncertainties and conflicting viewpoints. Examining our own beliefs about extraterrestrial life and contact invites us to reflect on how perspectives and beliefs shape our experiences and interpretations. Navigating the conflict between belief systems requires empathy, open-mindedness, and respectful communication. Self-reflection and preparation are vital, as they promote self-awareness, discernment, and emotional fortitude. Truly take the time to explore this topic, while being patient with yourself and seeking out resources and support when needed, all essential elements of a well-rounded and meaningful journey of exploration. Remember, this journey is highly individual, influenced by personal beliefs, experiences, and maturity, and it is important to engage in it at a pace that feels comfortable and meaningful to you.

Throughout the course of my life, I have accumulated a wealth of experiences that ultimately led me to this significant moment of contact. Each challenge I faced along the way has been alchemized into valuable gifts of self-love and heightened awareness. As I traversed my personal journey, I expanded the boundaries of my perceptions and bravely carved out my own unique path, which was driven by humility and the transformative power of suffering. It is essential to note that my personal encounters with extraterrestrials were far from intimidating or fear inducing. They were insistent upon establishing a connection with individuals who possess a mindset devoid of fear, and had heart resonance brimming with courage. Being aware of my human limitations and their methods of communication, I realize that the extraordinary experience I had was a result of the alignment between my heart and mind, and being in the perfect setting.

Contrary to some beliefs, their presence is not for the purpose of saving us from our plight. Engaging with humans in a manner that could potentially instigate a state of fear driven de-evolution serves no productive purpose. Such actions would directly contradict their mission of closely monitoring the evolution of our species. Their interactions are intended to serve as a catalyst for growth rather than inducing fear or anxiety. The ability to establish contact arose from a state of complete surrender to the moment, wherein I found myself immersed in deep meditation and engaged in active conscious awareness with my higher self. It was during this introspective state that I asked for assistance while maintaining a vibrational alignment with my higher self.

The process of alignment heightened my awareness, prompting me to recall various moments throughout my life that shed light on my true nature—coming from conscious light energy. I vividly remembered the experience of the radiant light energy from my father's passing. I also recognized the luminescence that I myself embodied, where the profile of my face emerged through a veil of light during a guided meditation in my astrology program, an eighteen-month immersion, deepening my relationship with the planets, houses, and energies of the angels. I also experienced an awareness in the moment of all the others who had come before me and I experienced their light as well. Many people have experienced encounters with their inner light, yet the vastness of these experiences makes it challenging to capture them all. These narratives are frequently dismissed as a part of near-death encounters, as the image of a light at the end of the tunnel is commonly associated with individuals in their final moments. Those who connect with their inner light through spiritual pathways are more extensively documented and recognized among the known instances, like Buddha or Yeshua, also known as Jesus. The light perceived and taught by Buddha and Yeshua, or during astral travel, is a manifestation of each individual's source of consciousness, transcending any distinctions among these experiences.

The words that flowed from my mouth harmoniously matched the circumstances and the vibrational field of my heart at that moment. As I continued my meditation, guided by my higher self, I was led toward releasing attachments in order to alleviate my suffering. I wholeheartedly surrendered to the recommendations provided by my higher self, embracing the evolutionary expedition that lay before me. In a bold move, I stepped out of my comfort zone and embarked on an unprecedented action—I humbly asked for my higher self's assistance and specifically requested her to reach out for help on my behalf. In my plea, I urged her to extend the request to anyone who could offer guidance, specifically other beings of light, all while thinking of my own light, as well as my father's light, in my mind and in my heart.

Following are some questions we can ask ourselves at any time to assess our current state of conscious awareness.

- How present am I in the present moment? Am I fully focused on right here and now, or are my thoughts consumed by the past or future worry?

- What is the quality of my thoughts? Are they predominately hopeful and empowering, or do they lean toward unfavorable and self-limiting?

- How connected do I feel to my emotions? Am I in touch with my feelings and able to express them authentically, or do I tend to suppress or ignore them?

- How open am I to new perspectives and ideas? Am I willing to challenge my beliefs and expand my understanding, or do I cling rigidly to preconceived notions?

- How aligned am I with my values and purpose? Am I living in accordance with what truly matters to me, or am I caught up in external expectations or societal conditioning?

- How mindful am I in daily activities? Do I approach tasks with full awareness and intention, or do I find myself going through the motions without true presence?

- How interconnected do I feel with others and the world around me? Do I cultivate empathy, compassion, and a sense of unity, or do I tend to operate from a place of separation and self-centeredness?

- How consciously do I make choices and take actions? Am I acting out of habit or compulsion, or am I intentionally responding based on inner wisdom and understanding?

- How attuned am I to my body and its needs? Am I practicing self-care and listening to the messages my body sends, or am I neglecting its well-being?

- How content and fulfilled do I feel in my life? Am I cultivating a sense of gratitude, joy, and purpose, or am I constantly seeking external validation or falling into patterns of dissatisfaction?

CHAPTER 2:
Getting on the Path—
Illuminating the Way

You are an extremely unique and valuable cutting-edge energy generator, an electric self-healing superhuman with immense potential, currently only operating at a small fraction of your true capabilities. However, you possess the capacity to broaden your horizons and explore new pathways to unlock exciting new abilities.

With a natural inclination to evolve alongside your host planet, you are constantly in a state of growth or recession, flowing or ebbing, as energy never remains stagnant. Energy is a dynamic two-way vibrational form, where giving does not always imply receiving the same. It can be transformed in various ways. Clarity in our energetic expressions enhances perception. We are all receivers and transmitters; everyone has the capacity to both receive and transmit energy because we are energetic beings. Some excel at picking up energy—receivers—while others proficiently transform received energy—transformers.

In astrological terms, the transformer energetic signature is associated with the eighth and twelfth houses, where individuals like me with five placements in the twelfth house, are labeled as having transformer energy. This is also amplified by the fact that my twelfth house is in Scorpio, my Sun sign. Scorpio rules the eighth house, which is also associated with transformation.

Each person acts as an energetic battery, generating, emitting, transforming, and receiving energy through various channels like thoughts, brain waves, heart energy, electromagnetic fields, and aura vibrations. Recognizing and tapping into this energy can help us remember our true nature and transform into higher forms of the intelligent, energetic beings we already are. Your purpose here is to evolve, and you are fulfilling it admirably. You are already, technically, manufactured intelligence. You were designed by a higher intelligence. Humans now are essentially imitating what we have seen from our creators, which is bringing forth another intelligent form of life. They are master creators, and we are merely operating at a fraction of their capacity. The existence of everything is essential for life to manifest in this unique manner on our planet. Your mission is to advance the development of your physical body, which you have been diligently doing and continue to do. You are also here to evolve your consciousness, and you are actively engaged in this process.

In addition to advancing our consciousness, we must also develop our heart's resonance. The heart serves as the gateway to unlocking personal evolution. It is essential to realize that the limitations imposed upon us are often shaped by society's norms. Once we break free from societal constraints and conditioned thinking, we can access and engage with our heart's true resonance. Connections built within our communities are forms of support and understanding.

Prioritizing self-interests or offering assistance solely for financial gain indicates a lingering influence of the capitalist mindset that has subjugated humanity. True evolution of consciousness and heart resonance involves transcending self-centered motives and recognizing our interconnectedness. Society typically promotes individualism, putting people against each other based on race, class, or gender, fostering divisions that detract from our shared humanity. The more we distance ourselves from one another, the harder it becomes to perceive the reflections of ourselves in others. Every individual holds inherent value, and those who selflessly contribute to the well-being of others often exhibit a higher level of consciousness than those solely driven by personal gain or material wealth.

Understanding your origin and recognizing that your physical form is merely a vessel is a key to unlocking your potential for evolution. Your body is like your spacesuit, as you have been evolving in harmony with this planet to ensure the survival of our species. Your consciousness functions as your operating system, and every individual plays a vital role in the development of our collective evolution of consciousness. At this moment in time, it may be difficult to fully grasp the profound possibilities that await humanity. However, both as individuals and as a species, as our awareness grows we begin to catch glimpses of the limitless potential within ourselves.

Creating higher levels of consciousness and exploring the depths of our minds and abilities stimulates an increase in brain synapses, which, in turn, leads to enhanced communication on a cellular level, triggering the release of neurotransmitters and facilitating literal cellular communication within our bodies. By tapping into these abilities, we unlock a cascade of synchronicities and open ourselves up to transformative experiences that imprint new memories within our DNA.

As creatures of habit, it is crucial for us to consciously be aware of our thought patterns and behaviors. Taking control of our habitual actions and adapting empowering behaviors allows us to rewire our brains, upgrading from outdated internal programming to newly updated systems and stored memories. This new way of thinking illuminates the path to our true selves and highest potential. Keep in mind that your intentions guide your behaviors. Over time, behaviors evolve into habits, and habits culminate in practice. As your practice matures, it seamlessly integrates into your nature, ultimately defining who you are.

Heightened awareness of our environment, abilities, and interconnectedness amplifies our power and potential. When we align ourselves with like-minded individuals, harmonizing our energies and intentions, the collective energy intensifies, creating a ripple affect of greater impact and manifestation. As we tap into the wellspring of our collective consciousness, we unlock hidden reservoirs of creativity, wisdom, and innovation. Together we become a force to be reckoned with, capable of shaping the trajectory of not only our own lives, but also the world around us. On this journey of personal and collective evolution, it is essential to remain open minded, embracing the infinite possibilities within and around us. Continuously expanding our awareness, exploring our natural abilities, and fostering unconditional loving connection to all living beings propels us forward on the path of self-realization.

By harnessing the power of conscious creation and intentional manifestation, we unleash the immense potential dwelling within us, igniting a transformative spark that sets ablaze our authentic selves and propels us toward our highest aspirations. Trust in the boundless capacity for growth and embrace the interconnectedness of our existence. Together with like-minded souls, united by a common purpose, we can create a world bursting with possibilities and boundless love.

If you are choosing to get on the path, then you should be familiar with some of the things needed in order to access the rainbow bridge to enlightenment, or to live in your light. These are all familiar terms that are essentially the same thing. They will mean something slightly different to each person, but there is no doubt they all lead to the same place. The mind–body–spirit connection forms the essential groundwork we must establish before ascending the ladder of conscious awareness. The concept of the body–mind–spirit connection recognizes the interdependent nature of our physical, mental, and spiritual well-being. It suggests that these three aspects of our being are intricately linked and influence one another.

Throughout history, various cultures and belief systems have acknowledged this connection and emphasized its significance for human health. The body–mind–spirit connection is based on the idea that our bodies, minds, and spirits are not separate entities but instead are integrated aspects of our being. It suggests that any imbalance or disharmony in one area can affect the others. This concept is rooted in ancient healing traditions such as Ayurveda, Traditional Chinese Medicine, and with indigenous clans' healing practices, which have long recognized the holistic nature of human health.

The physical aspect of the body–mind–spirit connection refers to our bodily health and well-being. It involves maintaining a balanced diet, engaging in regular exercise, and getting enough rest and sleep. Physical health is crucial for overall well-being, as it provides a solid foundation for mental and spiritual wellness. When we neglect our physical health, it can lead to various elements that unfavorably impact our mental and spiritual states.

The mental aspect of the body–mind–spirit connection focuses on our thoughts, emotions, and cognitive processes. Our mental well-being significantly influences our physical health and spiritual vitality. Stress, anxiety, and negative thought patterns can manifest as physical symptoms or contribute to the development of chronic illnesses. On the other hand, cultivating a positive mindset, managing stress effectively, and engaging in activities that promote mental wellness can enhance our overall health and vitality.

The spiritual aspect of the body–mind–spirit connection encompasses our sense of purpose, values, and connection to something greater than ourselves. It does not necessarily refer to religious beliefs but rather to our innermost essence and the search for meaning in life. Nurturing our spiritual well-being can contribute to improved mental and physical health. Practices like meditation, prayer, and spending time in nature can help us connect with our inner selves, find peace, and gain a deeper understanding of life.

Understanding the interplay between the body, mind, and spirit is crucial for achieving optimal health and well-being. For example, regular physical exercise not only strengthens our bodies, it also releases endorphins in the brain that uplift our mood and positively impact our mental state. Similarly, practicing gratitude in meditation can reduce stress levels and enhance our spiritual awareness while also positively affecting our physical health by reducing blood pressure and improving immune functions. Recognizing and nurturing the body–mind–spirit connection is essential for human health.

Holistic well-being: viewing health from a holistic perspective allows us to address and balance issues promoting well-being on multiple levels simultaneously. By acknowledging the interconnectedness of our physical, mental, and spiritual selves, we can adopt comprehensive approaches to self-care.

I understand that repetition is important for imprinting information. Therefore, I will reiterate information because it is crucial for us to grasp and internalize this knowledge. Remember, your intentions will shape your behaviors. Over time, your repeated behaviors turn into your habits, and these habits develop into your practice. As your practice matures, they will become an inherent part of your nature, ultimately shaping your identity. Developing a regular practice to support your journey toward well-being and self-discovery are the beginning steps of the path. Whether it is through yoga and meditation, journaling, or connecting with nature, establishing a consistent routine can have considerable influence on your physical, mental, and spiritual health. By dedicating time each day to these practices, you create a space for self-reflection, introspection, and personal fulfillment.

To develop a practice that suits your needs and preferences, there are a few key tips to keep in mind. First and foremost, dedicate a specific time each day that works best for you. This is where new AI technology can be incredibly useful. You can list your daily tasks and have AI create a detailed schedule for you, including yoga and meditation sessions, journaling, meal planning, cooking, and more. With AI, the more detail you provide, the better they can assist you. Whether it's managing chores or sticking to a diet plan, AI can help keep you on track for personal growth. You can even request specialized yoga programs, tailored to your needs and schedule. You might choose Pilates, simple stretching, or opt for a run. We don't need to all use the same methods; we can craft our own tools for physical, mental, and spiritual well-being; forging our own paths instead of following others. Essentially, AI can assist you with anything to maintain a consistent routine and enhance your self-improvement journey. Consistency is key, so aim for a time when you can commit to your practice without interruption. It may be early morning, during a lunch break, or before bed. Choose a time that aligns with your schedule and allows you to fully engage in the practice without rushing.

Next, find a quiet and comfortable space where you can focus and feel at peace. This could be a corner of your home, a peaceful park, or another cozy spot in nature. Creating an environment that supports your practice helps foster a sense of tranquility and deepen your connection to the activity. Experimenting with different techniques is such a fun part of the process. I maintain various spaces designated for different seasons and locations, each serving distinct purposes. I engage in a personal ritual practice to honor all the elementals, recognizing their vital role in enabling me to access the profound energy that allows me to communicate with animals, cultivate, and connect deeply with the land.

Communicating with the land is a deeply revered practice for me. My way of connecting with the land may differ significantly from another person's experience of connecting with the earth. The methods through which we show reverence to Mother Earth can vary greatly from individual to individual. There is no one-size-fits-all approach here when it comes to practices that nurture well-being and self-improvement. Try various meditation techniques such as visualizations and guided imagery, mindfulness and loving kindness, breath awareness alongside muscle relaxation, or affirmation meditations introducing mindset shifts to discover new pathways; always find what resonates within you. Of coarse, you don't actually need to do anything in your meditations; silence is one of the best tools we can utilize.

The value of silence in meditation is immeasurable. Silence in nature is both free and extremely rewarding. When we immerse ourselves in the silence of nature, we can explore the idea of losing our self-identity, embracing unity.

"Silence is the poetry of space." —Gordon Hempton

"Silence is not the absence of anything, but rather the presence of everything. In the presence of everything we disappear."
—Gordon Hempton

Through silence, we can listen to our inner voices and gain deeper insights where our thoughts are going, as well as the quality of our thoughts. Silence is a free tool that all are able to utilize. When we embrace moments of silence, it enables us to cultivate a rich inner conversation with ourselves and with the world around us.

Similarly, explore different journaling methods, such as gratitude journaling or stream of consciousness writing and reflective prompts. There are many styles of journaling, such as gratitude journaling, dream journaling, vision journaling, and healing journaling. Find the style that allows your thoughts and emotions to flow freely. We are well aware of the benefits of engaging in activities that we love in silence. Having the opportunity to immerse ourselves fully in our work—whether it's for professional reasons, personal hobbies, or passions—allows us to focus and perform at our best. Giving undivided attention to our projects enables us to excel in all of our endeavors.

Be open to exploring new practices beyond meditation and journaling. Spending time in nature, for instance, can be incredibly grounding and rejuvenating. Take regular walks or bike rides in the park, hike or bike in the mountains, or simply sit by a serene body of water. Gardening also provides a wonderful avenue for meditation, allowing us to connect with negatively charged grounding energies and communing with our nurturing Mother Earth energy. Nature has a way of calming our minds, rejuvenating our spirits, and fostering a sense of connection with the world around us.

Remember that developing a regular practice is a journey in itself. It requires commitment, patience, and self-compassion. Some days may be more challenging than others, and that's okay. Embrace the process, allowing yourself to grow and evolve along the way, knowing that the ebb and flow of energy in life will come naturally. Adapt your practice as needed, explore new techniques, and adjust your routine to fit your needs. Embrace the journey and stay open to exploration, allowing your practices to guide you toward a more balanced and fulfilling life. There is no time limit to these activities. These are lifetime accomplishments. For some it takes a lifetime to master stillness and become one with all that is. Others will be a lighthouse and know the path their entire life.

Once you have established a strong connection between your body, mind, and spirit, you begin to recognize patterns and cycles in nature that mirror the internal rhythms within you. Synchronicity's meaningful coincidences start to manifest, signaling that you are on the right path and doing the work. These signs can be found in everything and everyone around you, as every experience and every individual offers valuable lessons and teachings. Approaching life circumstances with a mindset of learning enriches your state of being and empowers you.

When you approach each person you encounter open to learn from them, you embrace an empowered way of living. Shifting from the roles of aggressor and victim to those of student and teacher signifies a heightened level of consciousness. The victim mentality is often promoted by society for division within our minds. Viewing situations as a type of personal attack is characteristic of a victim mindset. By taking things personally, you have assumed the role of victim. This mindset creates a divide between you and others. Even if the other person meant harm, it is only because of the their inability to see past their own pain. Moving past these types of actions involves embracing the present without focusing on the past. While pain and suffering are still a part of the human experience, undertaking inner work empowers us to transcend adversities and perceive them as valuable assets. Through a series of learned lessons and experiences, we eventually transition into a mindset where we view all encounters as opportunities for growth.

It is vital to understand that the cyclical nature of life reveals that both favorable and unfavorable times carry essential life lessons, with the latter offering profound insights due to the challenges they present. During peaceful and comfortable periods, we may not actively seek growth opportunities, but it is during times of adversity that our capacity for learning and evolution is truly tested. Embracing life's fluctuations is crucial for our development on Earth; stress and obstacles serve as catalysts for human development and strength. Every aspect of our lives contributes to our soul's journey, and with introspection and a holistic understanding of our path we can extract valuable lessons from every circumstance we encounter.

Another powerful tool at our disposal to aid in the journey toward our higher selves is unlocking and activating our chakra system, as with yoga. Much like the interconnectedness of the mind, body, and spirit, we can observe the tangible affects of our efforts within our physical bodies. The chakra system serves as a vital bridge and pathway, carrying the codes and information that shape our essence throughout our entire being. Unlocking and activating the chakras becomes a pivotal key to our conscious evolution, propelling us further along the path of self-discovery and personal growth.

Yoga is an ancient practice renowned for its ability to harmonize and align the body's energy systems. Developing and balancing our chakra system requires dedicated effort and self-exploration. As we dive into this transformative practice, we become more attuned to the energy centers within our bodies. Each chakra corresponds to specific aspects of our physical, emotional, and spiritual well-being. By consciously working on each chakra, we can dissolve energy blockages, restore harmony, and enhance the free flow of vital energy throughout our entire system.

Starting from the root chakra, which grounds us to the earthly realm, we gradually ascend through the chakras, allowing ourselves to experience a firm foundation and profound sense of connection and alignment with our higher selves. The sacral chakra nurtures our creativity, passion, and sensuality, while the solar plexus chakra empowers us to embrace our personal power and confidently manifest our desires. It is often referred to as the birthplace of our light. Moving further upward, the heart chakra is a portal and opens the gateway to love, compassion, and emotional healing, fostering deep connections with ourselves and others. The throat chakra facilitates authentic self-expression and effective communication, empowering us to speak our truth and convey our thoughts and feelings with clarity. The third eye chakra, our intuitive center, invites us to trust our inner wisdom, expand our awareness, and develop heightened spiritual insights. Finally, the crown chakra connects us to divine consciousness, allowing us to tap into limitless cosmic wisdom and experience a profound sense of unity with the universe.

Each chakra possesses a unique vibrational response and corresponds to specific hues and tones. Achieving balance and alignment within our chakra system varies between each individual, considering all aspects of one's being as a unified whole. In the realm of holistic health, we recognize the interconnectedness of every part without elevating any single aspect above the other. When working with our chakras, we strive to reach an elevated state of consciousness and being, compared to attaining a higher octave of self. To reach the higher state of self, we must first tune and balance the lower self. This journey involves navigating between the lower self state and the higher self state, aiming to expand our state of mind and existence. As we tune our body's chakras and exist in a state of oneness and wholeness, functioning harmoniously like a well-oiled machine, we are actively engaged in the process of evolution.

This is the ultimate goal—a state in which more individuals are attaining this heightened state of being. In this process, a domino effect unfolds, and the ripples of those vibrations and transformation create a new reality for all. It is crucial to recognize the significance of this message at present, as we navigate a time where it holds paramount importance for our collective awakening and co-creation of our new harmonious reality. When we collectively reach a state of active evolution, vibrating as one, the transformative effects ripple to humanity. This interconnected shift has the power to create a new reality, one that is marked by unity and compassion from an expanded consciousness. Now more than ever, it is essential to heed this message and actively engage in your own development as we contribute to the collective transformation and usher in a future of profound well-being. Just as in life, the ebb and flow of experiences serve as invaluable teachers, enabling us to develop and sharpen our skills.

Once we nurture the chakra system alongside our body–mind–spirit connection, some things tend to happen within us if we pay close enough attention. Undoubtedly we will be that attuned if we are actively engaged in our and the collectives evolutionary process. We develop a relationship with our inner self, which is when you trust in yourself, also known as intuition. Developing psychic abilities is a fascinating and interesting journey that opens up incredible possibilities for exploring the realms beyond the physical. The term *psychic* refers to *the intuitive capabilities that extend beyond the five senses, enabling individuals to perceive and interpret information through extrasensory perception (ESP), clairvoyance, clairaudience, or other psychic abilities.* While these abilities are often associated with mysticism and the supernatural, they are deeply rooted in our inherent spiritual and energetic nature. The development of psychic abilities begins with cultivating a heightened sense of self-awareness and expanding our consciousness. It requires a deep understanding that we are not just physical bodies but spiritual beings existing within a vast multi-dimensional universe. By embracing this understanding, and recognizing the interrelations of all things, we open ourselves up to the limitless potential of our psychic capabilities.

One of the first steps in developing psychic abilities is to silence the noise of the external world and tune into our inner selves. This involves dedicating time for introspection, meditation, and mindfulness practices. By quieting our minds and tuning into the present moment, we enhance our ability to perceive subtle impressions and messages from beyond our physical senses. The essential aspect of psychic development is trusting our intuition. Intuition serves as a profound and reliable compass, guiding us toward the truth and helping us make decisions aligned with our highest good. Learning to listen to our inner voice and to trust the messages it imparts is crucial for the development of psychic abilities. This requires cultivating a deep sense of self-trust and learning to discern between ego-based thoughts and intuitive guidance. Regular practice is essential in developing psychic abilities. By engaging in exercises that specifically target these skills, we strengthen our psychic muscles and enhance our innate abilities. These exercises may include activities such as sound baths, aura readings, Reiki energy healing, card readings, remote viewing, or psychic mediumship practices.

Regularly engaging in such practices heightens our sensitivity to energy and strengthens our psychic connections. Additionally, keeping a journal dedicated to documenting intuitive insights, dreams, synchronicities, and any psychic experiences can be immensely valuable. This allows us to reflect upon and track our progress, identify patterns and symbols, and gain a deeper understanding of our intuitive strengths and weaknesses.

It is important to note that the development of psychic abilities requires patience and perseverance. It is a process that develops over time, with varying levels of intensity and unique experiences for each individual. It is not a linear path, but rather an organic journey of self-discovery and spiritual growth. Maintaining a higher vibrational frequency through self-care practices is beneficial for psychic development. This can include engaging in activities that help lift and nourish our energy such as yoga, time in nature, practicing gratitude, engaging in creative pursuits, and staying physically, mentally, and emotionally balanced. Understanding and respecting our boundaries is also important while developing psychic abilities. It is crucial to honor our own energetic sovereignty and to discern what feels right and aligned with your highest good. Grounding practices such as spending time in nature, connecting with the earth, and practicing pranayama (breath work) can help maintain a solid foundation as we navigate the realms of psychic exploration.

Humility and ethical responsibility are also crucial aspects of developing psychic abilities. It is important to approach this journey with humility, acknowledging that psychic abilities are gifts to be used for the higher good of all. Practicing ethical guidelines such as obtaining permission from others before providing psychic readings and respecting privacy ensures that we use our abilities with integrity and compassion. Developing psychic abilities is an enriching and transformative journey that taps into the deep well of our spiritual nature. Through inner work, meditation, regular practice, self-care, and a strong commitment to personal growth, we can expand our intuitive capacities and build a greater connection to the realms beyond the physical. Embracing these abilities with humility, ethical responsibility, and a dedication to the highest good allows us to co-create a more fulfilling and connected existence, enriching both our own lives and the lives of those we encounter.

Since humanity's next evolutionarily leap in consciousness will encompass the development of sensory perception, almost like acquiring superpowers, we need to be vigilant on our path. Remarkably, such abilities are already being nurtured on our planet. While some may be unaware of their endeavors, others are already consciously cultivating these faculties. Contrary to common belief, emotions are not obstacles; they are in fact pivotal for elevating the human heart to new heights. By tapping into emotions and nurturing empathy for humanity, we unlock our innate sensory perceptions. The psychic abilities will manifest uniquely for each of us based on individuals' astrological and energetic imprints.

From an astrological perspective, we are currently undergoing a cosmic shift in energy as we enter into the Aquarian Era, represented by the Water Bearer, which is an air sign. This current shift in energy is leading to a widespread awakening to our surroundings. As we journey through the cosmos, the dynamics of power and influence are evolving. By aligning ourselves with the present energies and what they offer, we actively elevate our consciousness, tuning ourselves to the opportunities of the moment.

Air signs are associated with the intellect, focusing on mental faculties. Aquarius, a sign emphasizing individuality and amicability, features the Water Bearer, signifying creation and the free flow of life. The water in the symbol signifies the unrestrained truth streaming from the vessel, mirroring our emotions that pour forth as water from our essence. In moments of heightened emotion, we are said to be entrenched in our authenticity, a significant milestone unfolding in this collective movement toward embracing and standing in our truth. As we witness the commencement of the Aquarian Era, characterized by emotional solidarity and a unified front, challenging establishments that neglect both people and planet, we stand poised on the cusp of transformative change—characteristic of the Aquarius sign. By tapping into these powerful emotions, we find our authentic self. Authenticity is at the core of our connectivity for the energies around us at all times.

The variety of psychic abilities is vast, and each person may have a different combination of these abilities. The kinds of ESP emerging from self-actualized humans will vary, and new abilities will continue to emerge as we evolve. Some of the most commonly recognized psychic abilities as of today include the following.

- Telepathy: The ability to perceive thoughts and emotions of others.

- Clairvoyance: *Clear seeing;* the ability to perceive information about a person, object, or event.

- Clairaudience: *Clear hearing;* the ability to perceive sounds or messages beyond the physical range of human hearing.

- Clairsentience: *Clear feelings;* the ability to feel beyond physical realm such as emotions, energies, or the vibrations of others.

- Claircognizance: *Clear knowing;* ability to receive knowledge or insights without any prior information or logical reasoning. Understanding and answers seem to just "drop in" to their awareness.

- Telekinesis: The ability to manipulate objects with the mind.

- Precognition: The ability to perceive future events before they happen.

- Psychometry: The ability to perceive information about an object or its owner by touching it.

These abilities are thought to be innate, but some individuals may not be aware of their psychic potential or may have under-developed abilities. Understanding one's astrological birth chart can provide insight into the potential psychic modality a person may be attuned to, based on the positions of celestial bodies at the time and place of their birth. Astrology is the study of the positions and movements of celestial bodies in relation to human affairs and natural events. An astrological birth chart, also known as a natal chart, is a map of the celestial coordinates at the exact time, date, and place of a person's birth. It consists of the positions of the sun, moon, planets, and other astrological points in the zodiac. In astrology, certain celestial placements are believed to influence psychic abilities and tendencies. For example, the position of Neptune in a person's chart is often associated with heightened intuition, empathy, and sensitivity to the unseen. Neptune is the planet of psychic visions, imagination, spirituality, creativity, and mystery or the hidden. Neptune is known as the planet of dreams and the ability to perceive things beyond the physical realm. Likewise, Mercury, the planet of communication, may influence telepathic abilities in the capacity to perceive and understand nonverbal forms of communication.

Additionally, the twelve astrological signs and their associated elements—fire, earth, air, and water—may provide further insight into a person's psychic potential. For instance, significant water placements and signs such as Pisces, Cancer, and Scorpio are often regarded as highly intuitive and empathic, while air placements and signs like Gemini, Libra, and Aquarius may exhibit strong abilities in communication and mental perception. Dominant Earth placements may excel in psychometry, whereas dominant fire placements and fire signs can be energetic movers, potentially linked to telekinesis. By exploring their astrological birth chart, individuals can gain a deeper understanding of their psychic inclinations and potential strengths. This insight can serve a starting point for developing their psychic talents. For example, someone with a strong Neptune placement might benefit from practices that enhance intuition such as meditation, dream journaling, and energy work. Meanwhile, an individual with prominent Mercury influences might focus on developing telepathic abilities through mental exercises and visualization techniques.

It's important to note that while astrology can offer insightful perspectives, developing psychic abilities requires dedication, practice, and an open mind. Regardless of astrological influences, honing your gifts often involves self-discovery, personal growth, and a willingness to explore the mysteries of the mind–body–spirit connection.

The journey toward finding the path to one's highest self is a highly individualized experience. It manifests differently for each person, and is guided by their unique personality and preferences. As individuals embark on this quest, they will naturally gravitate toward various healing modalities that are accessible, readily available, and resonate with their inner being. These diverse modalities serve as tools for our personal growth and transformation, allowing each individual to explore and embrace the methods that align most closely with their own journey. Our astrological birth charts hold immense value as constant points of reference for seeking guidance and deeper understanding in our lives. Unfortunately, many have dismissed astrology as a superficial and nonsensical pseudoscience.

However, in truth it contains keys to personal growth and self-improvement for each individual. It can unlock answers and broaden our understanding of ourselves. Humanity has been observing the stars ever since they began writing language. Our earliest writings documented our celestial discoveries, as we swiftly recognized our interconnectedness with the cosmos and how the planets' energies impacted our existence. This awareness prompted us to diligently track and record these cosmic influences. It is vital for each person to comprehend their own birth chart due to the abundance of people on the Internet offering astrological weather reports. Many try to fit themselves into someone else's interpretation of the astrological energies at any given time.

Traditionally, our HolyDays (holidays) have always been linked to astrological occurrences, which is why celestial events are commemorated globally in some form. However, the transformation of each holy day into a marketing ploy has unfortunately become normalized in modern times. When you seek understanding of yourself from external sources, it reflects a deficiency in your self-awareness. Seeking another person's perspective on your self is inherently limited and biased by their outlook. A prime illustration would be someone who never grasped the significance of Mercury retrograde because they never experienced any disruptions in their own communications or life during those periods. It is highly likely that they possess strong mercury placements, perhaps even being born during Mercury retrograde themselves. However, without this awareness, one may not comprehend how certain phenomenon affects them or why others may not. Engaging in your own work yields the most authentic answers and optimal results. Relying on external sources for this purpose is merely a manifestation of capitalism.

It is crucial to recognize that each person's perspective is different and is based on their own unique planetary alignment, childhood experiences, and natural capacity. Each personal story will naturally vary as individuals interpret and navigate their birth charts, with each chart as unique as fingerprints. The state of being, the emotions, and the energy with which one approaches this work greatly influences the outcomes and experiences. Whatever state of being one is in while doing this work becomes the foundation for the work itself. By recognizing the profound connection between energy, astrology, and our own personal journeys, we have the potential to become our own astrological meteorologists, predicting and interpreting our own personal astrological weather reports, which are much more in tune with our own personal journey. You alone have the capacity to truly comprehend the significance of your planetary placements on your journey, empowering yourself along the way.

Life is filled with challenges and obstacles that can test our resilience, determination, and ability to adapt. While these hurdles may feel overwhelming at times, it is important to remember that they present opportunities for growth and self-discovery. By developing effective strategies and cultivating a resilient mindset, we can navigate challenges and overcome obstacles with confidence. Adopting an assured mindset is crucial when facing challenges. Cultivate an optimistic outlook that focuses on solutions rather than dwelling on the problem. Train your mind to see the setbacks as opportunities for growth and learning, and to believe in your ability to overcome all obstacles. Clearly define your goals and break them down into manageable steps. This approach helps you maintain focus and direction even in the face of adversity.

By taking small actionable steps towards your goals, you build momentum and gradually overcome obstacles. Flexibility and adaptability are key when navigating challenges. Life doesn't always go according to plan and unexpected obstacles can arise, usually because we have something we need to learn. Embrace change, and be willing to adjust your strategies and approaches as needed. Adapting to new circumstances allows you to find alternative solutions and move forward.

Don't be afraid to reach out for support when facing challenges. Seek guidance from mentors, trusted friends, or family members who can offer valuable perspectives and advice. Sharing your struggles with others not only provides emotional support but also opens up opportunities for collaboration and problem solving. Genuine engagement with others about oneself should be a cooperative open exchange—a dialogue involving questions and answers with trusted people who are not solely focused on financial gain, such as friends or family members. If money alone could solve all of our problems, then why do so many wealthy people still struggle? Those unable to afford paid solicitation and advice are left without options. If society insists on a model where people must pay for help and many cannot afford it, how can we progress? Where can those without the financial means find guidance to address their challenges?

Resilience is the ability to bounce back from setbacks and persevere in the face of challenges. Cultivate resilience by reframing failures as learning experiences, nurturing self-belief, and developing healthy coping mechanisms such as mindfulness, self-care, and seeking social support. Failure is an inevitable part of life, and it provides valuable lessons for growth opportunities. Instead of viewing failure as a setback, see it as a steppingstone to success. Analyze what went wrong and learn from your mistakes, and then use that knowledge to make better-informed decisions in the future. Engaging in the analysis of your mistakes to make better-informed decisions for your future reflects an active pursuit of wisdom. Recognizing patterns and learning from their lessons is crucial on the path to success.

Perseverance is another key when overcoming obstacles. It is important to remember that success often requires time and effort. Stay committed to your goals, even when faced with setbacks. Stay persistent, adapt your approach if necessary, and keep pushing forward. Be kind and compassionate toward yourself during challenging times. Acknowledge that setbacks and obstacles are a natural part of the journey. Treat yourself with understanding, practice self-care, and remind yourself of your strengths and past successes. Instead of fixating on problems, shift your focus and find solutions. Take a proactive approach, brainstorm creative ideas, and explore different perspectives. By focusing on solutions, you empower yourself to take control and overcome your obstacles.

Celebrate your achievements no matter how small they may seem. Recognize and appreciate the progress you have made, as it boosts your confidence and motivates you to keep going. Each step forward is a victory worth acknowledging. Navigating challenges and overcoming obstacles requires a combination of flexibility, adaptability, and a positive mindset. By setting clear goals, seeking support, and practicing self-compassion while staying persistent, you can tackle challenges head on and emerge stronger on the other side. Remember that every obstacle is an opportunity for growth, and with determination and perseverance you can navigate life's waters and arrive at your desired destination.

For many years, I identified myself as a witch, and I still hold this opinion to some extent. I hold the idea that we all possess a connection to magic, because everything is energy and we are all energetic beings; we are either harnessing the energy around us or the energy around us is influencing us. I perceive inherent magical energy within all aspects of existence. Arthur C. Clarke said, "Magic is only science we don't understand yet." The word *yet* in the sentence is the focal point. It is clear that our scientific knowledge is constantly progressing. Practices that our ancestors once viewed as magical have now been validated through scientific methods and data analysis. Believing that we have reached the pinnacle of our scientific understanding would be short sighted, especially considering the current global situation. Observing the world around us reveals not a peak of achievement but rather a glaring despair of our shortcomings and challenges.

As we evolve, so will our science, and so will our understanding of energy and magic. When we consider western medicine as an example, we often overlook its full scope. We tend to focus solely on the benefits it provides without considering the origins of this knowledge. The foundation was made by the pioneers of medicine who, despite their discoveries leading to favorable effects, also engaged in questionable practices throughout history in the name of scientific progress. Science and medicine have evolved significantly from their primitive origins.

I consider myself now more of an Evolved Witch, and possess a deep understanding of energy operations. Evolved witches have honed their abilities to tap into various energies and harmoniously balance the vibrations that are accessible at all times. Mastering their own energy and connecting with the energies around them, they are able to manifest their intentions and bring about desired outcomes. The evolved witch knows that every word uttered is a spell cast into energetic vibrational form. The evolved witch knows the key to transformation lies in recognizing one's own energy, mindset, and state of being as the true sources of the magic they harness in existence. The evolved witch recognizes the vast potential within the energetic realm and utilizes this knowledge to bring about positive change and alignment with the universal forces. The evolved witch recognizes that the term *witch* was historically used as a derogatory term for those who didn't understand what owning your own true power meant, and is merely a term crafted by those who failed to grasp the depth of authenticity and the empowerment it embodies. The evolved witch sees witchcraft as a tool for healing, empowerment, and positive change in both their lives and in the world around them. The evolved witch knows that energy is the underlying essence of life, and uses it for everyday magical operations. When you tap into the very essence of life itself, what else do you need?

In the present day, capitalism has taken center stage. It is essential to teach and emphasize that a magician's true ability relies primarily on their internal landscape and inherent capabilities. It is by nurturing and developing these inner resources that one can truly harness the power of magic, rather than relying solely on external elements or tools. When a practitioner gives power to their tools but doesn't utilize their actual greatest tool, which is themselves, then the entire magical act will bring about different desired results.

This is where you will find humans stuck in their cycles of spell-casting that get them nowhere, but they keep doing the exact same thing without receiving what they think they want. If you aren't connecting to the energetic vibration of what you want, then you aren't really connecting to what you want. When casting spells, it is crucial to center your focus on yourself and your environment. Many people accidentally create new and usually unfavorable karma from the spells they cast. Spells are energetic links, and they become heavy karma if attached to others or certain objects. Connect with the vibrational frequency of what you desire and align your life accordingly. Remember, your words hold the power of spells each day, in every moment. Utilize them wisely and consciously. The fastest route to diminishing your own power is by repeating a spell crafted by someone else. Honing your craft is a talent that takes years, really a lifetime, because it should change, grow, and evolve just like everything else does. As above, so below.

The most noticeable difference I see between various magical individuals and their manifestations is that the less you talk about what you're doing, the more powerful your ability to manifest becomes, and the more you dilute yourself online, the less you actually manifest. This awareness can help you recognize how much energy you spend on being diluted in the digital space. When your magic is strong, it remains undiluted, allowing you to release its full potency in divine timing. However, it is easy to dilute yourself by trying to go with the flow and constantly entice people through marketing strategies, which diminish your effectiveness. If you attempt to fit into everyone else's categories, you lose your own identity. By showing up authentically and unapologetically in your true power, you will attract what is meant for you while maintaining a state of sovereignty.

Authenticity encompasses more than just love or the light within you; it involves honoring all energetic frequencies and maintaining balance. When you embrace authenticity, you fully accept yourself—including both favorable and unfavorable qualities. While we strive to express ourselves in loving ways, authenticity also means acknowledging the parts of us that experience all of our emotions, when it is warranted. It doesn't imply that we should be passive or just let it go in every situation. Being authentic means genuinely owning and expressing our emotions. When we are authentic, we apologize sincerely, love wholeheartedly, and allow ourselves to be vulnerable in all aspects of life; we just stop worrying about what others will say or how they will judge us. Authenticity includes the messiness of everything that makes us human, connecting with all facets of ourselves. The light represents the part that honors our journey and serves as a vehicle for our souls, which recognize the many universal laws at play in our lives.

Love is an energetic frequency that comprises various components, and every energetic frequency is multifaceted. Since love is such a complex frequency that encompasses so many facets, it will often reflect in both nurturing and challenging aspects within our lives. Most people associate love with warmth and support, but it also manifests in ways that others perceive as hurtful, especially when we attempt to protect ourselves out of love, or to protect others from pain. These protective instincts can lead to misunderstandings and conflict within relationships, demonstrating that love isn't always straightforward. Understanding this complexity allows us to navigate the deeper layers of love, recognizing that even the harder facets of love are still a powerful force for restorative recovery. Tough love, rooted in authenticity, involves genuinely expressing care while holding others accountable for their actions, even if it feels uncomfortable. A perfect example would be a mother's tough love. It embodies the perfect balance of nurturing and accountability, as she guides her children toward growth and resilience while also ensuring that they understand the importance of responsibility and discipline.

When we embrace authenticity, we aim to tap into everything that makes us whole, aiding our evolution and expanding our conscious awareness. Most judgments come from a place of non-acceptance. When we fully accept ourselves, the opinions of others lose their significance. We achieve this self-acceptance through authenticity. Judgments typically arise due to someone else's absence of self-love, lack of understanding, or refusal to accept that there are different ways to be beyond their own perspective. When we stop worrying about the judgments and comparisons of others, we empower ourselves to know that we are sovereign and whole, regardless of what anyone else thinks, says, or does. If someone chooses to judge us, it reflects their own lack of understanding rather than our worth. By embracing authenticity and recognizing that other people's judgments often reflect their own struggles, we can heal our own energy and open ourselves to learning about the various energy-healing modalities that support our journey toward self-actualization.

Energy-healing modalities are very common, and western medicine has just begun to recognize their actual potential and usefulness in the medical field. Below are a few types of modalities in the energy-healing field, and the main ones I have used on my healing journey. There is a plethora of information available to you for free on the Internet about every one of these subjects. On this journey, it is important to work within the modalities you are drawn to the most.

- Reiki: Originally a Japanese technique that involves the practitioner channeling healing energy through their hands to promote relaxation, stress reduction, healing, moving stuck energy, and overall well-being.

- Yoga: A holistic practice that originated in India, focused on integrating the body, mind, and spirit. It combines a variety of physical postures and movements (Asanas), breathing techniques (pranayama), meditation, and ethical principles for a life of wellness.

- Acupuncture: An ancient Chinese practice that involves inserting thin needles into specific points on the body to balance the flow of energy in the body, known as Qi, and promote healing.

- Crystal Healing: The use of crystals and gemstones to restore energetic balance, clear blockages, and enhance the flow of energy in the body.

- Chakra Healing: Focuses on balancing the seven main energy centers, or chakras, in the body to promote physical, emotional, and spiritual well-being.

- Sound Healing: Utilizes sound vibrations such as singing bowls, gongs, or chanting to restore harmony and balance in the energy system.

- Quantum Healing: Based on the principles of quantum physics, which involve using intention, visualization, and energy techniques to facilitate healing on a quantum level.

- Pranic Healing: A non-touch energy-healing system that involves the treatment of prana, or life force energy, to facilitate transformation of physical, emotional, and mental processes.

- Meditation: The most common and easily accessible healing modality, it is a practice involving stillness, silence, and focusing the mind on different things to promote a state of mental clarity, emotional calmness, and relaxation.

- Aromatherapy: Utilizes aromatic essential oils derived from plants to promote physical, emotional, and spiritual well-being. These oils are often inhaled, applied topically, or used in conjunction with massage to harness their therapeutic properties.

There are many modalities to choose from, so find the ones that suit you the best and use them together for a balanced, holistic healing experience.

Energy-healing experiences have left a profound imprint on my life, creating some of the most unforgettable moments I've ever experienced.

Each healing experience I encountered played a significant role in my self-awareness journey, serving as steppingstones along my healing path. One memorable instance took place during my time in college thirteen years ago, when I was studying holistic health and integrative medicine. In a class called Healing Touch, I was in a sub-group of four to five individuals and we utilized intuition to identify each others' issues and provide healing through energy channeling. I vividly recall a young woman in my group who lay on the table. As we went around in a circle, each offering their intuitive insights, prompted by our teacher, two classmates provided logical answers considering her age and limited life experiences. However, when it was my turn, I intuitively sensed her when she was two years old and identified abandonment as her core issue. Overwhelmed with emotion, she confirmed that her father had left her at that age and her life had since been challenging, accompanied by her mother's struggle as a single parent. Praised by the teacher for my accuracy, we directed our focus toward her healing journey. I had tapped into the emotions residing in her heart. It is a common practice for empaths, but I was unaware of my capabilities at the time. This experience taught me the importance of listening to emotions in the body, and it unveiled my aptitude as an empath.

It was through such real life practice during school that I began to recognize and understand the extent of my empathic talents. It wasn't until I reached nearly forty years of age that I truly embraced and believed in my empathic abilities. Reflecting on my past interactions with individuals in my life, I realized that I had an inclination toward connecting with others who were broken or struggling, a common side effect of being human. At the time, I was on my own healing journey, focused on fixing myself rather than attempting to help others.

Consequently, I struggled with being a supportive friend to those who were not interested in their own healing. Being an empath meant naturally gravitating toward emotionally damaged individuals, as my inherent desire was to heal the energies of those who seemed disconnected from self-love, because I also wanted to embody self-love. I yearned to help, and believed that if I loved them enough they would start to love themselves, which in turn would result in them loving me back. Since I did not posses self-love, I could not give it.

However, I learned a difficult lesson: That no one can be compelled to heal themselves unless they genuinely want to. Any efforts made on behalf of someone who is not ready for healing can be perceived as superiority, triggering a victim response. Most people react defensively when receiving unsolicited help, unaware of their actual needs. It is important to remember that each person's healing journey is their own responsibility. You are not accountable for anyone else's healing process. Empaths often find themselves drawn to individuals in need of healing and this dynamic requires careful navigation. It is crucial to be mindful of both your energies and those of others, understanding how they can impact each of you.

As a part of my holistic health program, I obtained certification in healing touch, and Reiki, which has become one of my preferred energy-healing modalities. I had the opportunity to practice these crafts during a business trip to Jamaica. Since authenticity is my natural state, my approach to these encounters was without pretense. During the trip a Coptic leader, who had been traveling with us, expressed feeling unwell and mentioned a severe headache. We were on a bus at a time, on a long journey with no immediate relief in sight, and I could sense her discomfort. Offering my assistance, I asked if there was anything I could do. I mentioned Reiki, asked if she knew of the practice, then asked if she would like me to have a session with her. Enthusiastically, she agreed, perhaps not expecting my immediate assistance. She had heard of Reiki and had been eager to try it out. Taking advantage of pressure points on her head and her feet, I worked to alleviate her headache by clearing energy blockages. She was initially hesitant about me touching her feet, but I explained that our nerves are connected in the feet, making it an effective area to work on, plus her feet were accessible because she only wore sandals. By focusing on these pressure points and shifting the blocked energy, she experienced instant relief. However, since we were on the bus I encountered difficulty grounding the displaced energy from her system. In that moment, she witnessed me absorbing her headache pain. Everyone on the bus was able to witness this unique occurrence, an aspect of the healing process that is often unseen.

Reiki sessions are commonly conducted in private, fostering a one-on-one environment between the practitioner and the recipient. The practitioner is skilled in safely channeling and guiding energy, with access to open sources to ground and release any displaced energy from the session. Usually Reiki practitioners are meticulous to avoid taking on the energy they aim to heal in others. They actively remove any residual energy from healing sessions to prevent absorbing the issues of others. Following the bus ride, the woman I helped opened up to me in such a loving way. She expressed her desire to talk further with me, and later that evening we were warmly welcomed into their home for a meal. I had the opportunity to meet her beloved family, and she shared with them what I had done for her.

As we gathered together, conversations turned toward business dealings. I sensed the tension in the room and respectfully excused myself from the discussion, feeling the need for a change of atmosphere. To my surprise, a few of the others followed me out, eager to ask questions about the earlier bus incident and seeking my opinion on the entire deal and people involved. All I could offer them was authenticity and my honest perspective. Once we left their compound, the group I had traveled to Jamaica with expressed their joy, emphasizing how my authenticity had proven to be the winning factor of the day.

Embracing your authentic self is the pathway to speaking and connecting with the divine source of consciousness that unites us all. Your authentic self resonates on a multi-dimensional level, vibrating with the essence of who you truly are. Authenticity serves as a crucial key on our individual journeys, unlocking the dormant potential within us all. As we navigate through life, there are various keys that lay dormant within us, but it is through authenticity that we are able to unlock and activate the other keys along our path. Authenticity can be intimidating for many people, as it requires embracing vulnerability on a profound level. When you wholeheartedly embody your authentic self, it is no longer about pleasing others but about staying true to your own essence. This may not attract a multitude of superficial friendships, but it will instead draw in the right kind of connections. Those who genuinely love and respect you for who you are will enter your life. If your authenticity scares others to the point where they can no longer be authentic around you, it is essential to accept it and discern the importance of the relationship.

In today's society, people often tie their authenticity to a brand they need to market, causing them to view themselves as commodities. This shifts their focus toward financial gain, thereby disconnecting them from their true selves and their authentic spiritual needs. There are several keys to unlocking your authenticity. First, you need a true self-reflective experience in which you take the time to understand what your values, beliefs, and emotions are and how they have shaped you. Second, you need honest communication. You must be truthful in your interactions with others and express your thoughts and feelings openly. Fearing what others might think prohibits your authentic self from emerging. Third, you must embrace vulnerability. By overcoming the fear of what others might think of you, you have become vulnerable, which will lead to deeper connections with yourself and with others. Fourth, follow your passions and engage in activities that you truly resonate with and bring you the most joy. This absolutely helps you align with your authentic self. Another key that unlocks your authentic self is setting boundaries. When you establish boundaries that respect your needs and values, you help protect your authenticity and well-being. Practicing self-care includes taking care of your physical, emotional, and mental well-being. Prioritize activities that nurture and support those authentic parts of yourself. Embracing your imperfections means that you understand that being authentic doesn't mean being perfect. Embrace your flaws and imperfections as your own unique identity. The diversity of life is what is needed, so embracing your imperfections and accepting ourselves fully is key. Finally, we must seek growth constantly, because being open to learning and growing is how we embrace new experiences and challenges that help us evolve on our journey.

I have developed a strong awareness of the potentially harmful nature of marketing in the spiritual world. In this world dominated by capitalistic entrepreneurs, marketing has emerged as a powerful tool transforming everything into a commodity. Its aim is to find what can be exploited, manipulated, and turned into sales, regardless of the person's need for them. Thus, marketing becomes a mechanism of manipulation, exerting pressure on individuals to buy products or services that they do not truly require. Goods and services for sale are not the same as spiritual altruism and the pursuit of connecting with Divine Energy, God and Goddess, masculine and feminine energies. Your connection cannot be purchased; it can only be cultivated through your own efforts.

A healthy capitalistic system has boundaries. Those boundaries will coincide with humanity's boundaries. Or at least they should. We live in a day and age where priests sit on gold thrones praying for starving children and billionaires are made by monopolizing markets, because this is an unbalanced capitalistic system, also known as hyper-capitalism. When everyone is working toward the same unbalanced capitalistic endeavors, then there is no more progress to be made. More of the same is just more of the same and it is a never-ending cycle—a rat race—that you will never be able to come out if you don't rise above it. If you can see that true humanity is seen on the poorest, not richest, you have found your path toward your higher self.

In the story of Yeshua (whom many began calling Jesus), sharing and spreading his light, he preached among the prostitutes and the lepers, condemning the merchants at the spiritual temples. Those who need help should receive help, but what he preached about more than 2000 years ago is not what is being preached about nor produced and taught today. Anyone can wear a crown and adorn themselves with jewelry, clothes, and make-up to project an external image. Priests and priestesses dress for a role, status, and personal affirmation. But what does their internal landscape naturally reflect? Who are they in quiet reflection when their needs are fulfilled? If needs are satisfied, what drives their desire for more? Is it merely a response to today's standards? If the standards contribute to an unbalanced system, it's evident that fundamental changes are needed. Anyone on the path of spirituality and striving to connect with their higher self while sharing goodness within the world is already a priest or a priestess, in essence. A piece of paper does not define a person; if you live in this way, no one else can tell you what you are. Your actions serve as a direct link to your true self. If your words do not align with your actions, then those words hold no meaning. No external program can define what you inherently are or aren't—your actions always reveal the truth.

Embracing my authenticity has led me to witness countless beautiful moments unfold along my path. Yet, when I have the opportunity to witness someone else embracing and utilizing authenticity's truth—receiving their own blessings from it—it fills me with even more hope and joy. It serves as a reminder that authenticity holds the power to awaken hope within others and allows them to tap into the incredible potential that resides within, embracing their true selves. There was a pivotal moment that profoundly impacted both my life and that of my partner. As his career reached new heights and his acclaim brought him tremendous success, he found himself in a compelling situation facing a week filled with apprehension. He opened up to me about the conflicting dynamics within a crucial business deal, where his company's prosperity relied heavily upon his abilities. Uncertain of which direction to proceed with the people involved, he asked for my guidance, although he already anticipated my response. It sparked a laugh from me, because he knew what I was going to say. In fact, he answered his own question, echoing the same sentiment I shared—the only way to move forward was with unwavering honesty and clarity. If those crucial elements were absent in the situation, then it was clear that he needed to step away. The situation boiled down to a simple black-and-white choice: Endure a plethora of unnecessary complications solely for the potential of monetary gain, or leave and opt for a different environment where he felt comfortable to truly achieve success. After all, the only rewards that could be obtained were built from his own proprietary knowledge, so wouldn't it be far more preferable to venture into a space of trust, rather than subject himself to doubt? Upon his return for the weekend, he collapsed to his knees before me, clenching my hands as tears swelled up in his eyes. With profound emotion, he exclaimed, "I see you, Mama! I truly see you!"

He went on to share the life-altering incident that had unfolded. Uncertain of how to navigate the meeting, he followed my advice, simply because he did not know what else to do. By choosing vulnerability and owning his position in that pivotal business gathering, he inadvertently introduced a trust factor that resonated with the group. As a result, they bestowed upon him the best position on the board, recognizing the authenticity and trust he brought forth. It is through such authenticity, the courage to truly be oneself in the presence of others, and the willingness to embrace personal truth instead of seeking approval that the seeds of trust are sown. Witnessing the profound outcomes that arise from the magic of authenticity, he began to truly comprehend the transformative power that emerges when we align ourselves with truth. It allowed him to see clearly the possibilities that can manifest when we attract from a place of genuine sincerity and integrity.

Being authentic is currently one of the most daunting challenges for humans on this planet. Others may exploit our vulnerabilities to inflict harm due to their own pain. When we embark on our healing journey, we realize that we have a choice to respond with hurt or not. Most of us are guilty of this at some point. We understand that others' actions stem from their own pain, as ours once did. Perhaps holding compassion for those in pain can disrupt the cycle, and embracing authenticity fully comes from recognizing that the victim mentality is a choice. Many people's reluctance to display their authentic selves stems from a fear of vulnerability, and it is fear that often holds them back. If individuals could grasp the boundless possibilities that await them beyond fear's grasp, we will all be courageously leaping into the realms of trust and surrender.

Trust and surrender are the gateways to experiencing magic, also known as energy, unfolding around us at all times. By releasing our fears, we embrace trust and willingly surrender to the flow of life. We surrender to the profound influences of the universe, opening ourselves to whatever unfolds, knowing it is for our highest good and the greater good of the universe. This is precisely why it is of such paramount importance to confront our shadows. When we illuminate our shadows with light, we discover that there is truly nothing to fear.

Below are some questions to consider on your personal growth.

- How have your personal experiences and challenges contributed to your personal growth?

- In what specific areas of your life have you noticed significant growth and transformation?

- How do you actively seek out opportunities for personal growth and self-improvement?

- Can you identify any limiting beliefs or patterns that have hindered your personal growth, and what steps have you taken to overcome them?

- How do you measure or track your progress in terms of personal growth, and what indicators or milestones do you use to evaluate your growth journey?

- Who has been a teacher for you? Is your relationship with them the same now as it was then, or did you learn later what value that relationship had?

- Have you referenced your birth chart and located similar aspects of it and your life as of now?

- What has been the biggest lesson you have learned as of today about love?

- What does the term *true love* mean to you? How do you show true love in your life, from your viewpoint of its meaning?

- Can you identify any attachments in your life that are hindering your growth, such as thoughts, people, things, or ideologies?

CHAPTER 3:
The Dark Matters—Facing Your Shadow

This is a transformative journey toward reaching our highest selves. Realizing we have to face our shadows and cross the depths of the dark void to find our true light should not instill fear in the hearts of those willing to go the distance. It requires dedication, effort, and the willingness to go above and beyond to discover our inner light and become a guiding beacon for the world. Instead of being daunting, this journey should be eagerly anticipated as, deep down, we acknowledge the need for this growth and evolution. It is a time for introspection and contemplation, a time to replenish our energy, as the process can sometimes be draining.

Just as roots of a plant begin to sprout and grow in the darkness of earth's soil, our own personal growth often starts in the most challenging and obscure dark places. Throughout our lives, we have formed attachments and connections, some of which may no longer serve our highest good. Letting go of these deeply ingrained aspects can be difficult, especially if they have been with us for a significant portion of our lives. Yet, it is through shadow work that we gain a profound understanding of ourselves, creating space for illuminating the hidden aspects of our subconscious. But what exactly is the shadow, and how can we approach and integrate it into our lives without feeling overwhelmed by fear or resistance? If the path to our highest self and ultimate happiness is represented by the light, then the shadow can be interpreted as the obstacles that prevent us from reaching the state of being fully happy. The concept is deceptively simple, but by maintaining this simplistic perspective while we confront the issues that block the path to our true selves, we can navigate the shadows with greater ease and clarity. Shadow work involves identifying and removing the obstacles or limitations that hinder our progress, obstructing our view of a fulfilling and loving life.

Our perspective can become distorted or clouded—equivalent to the shadow effect—when we hold onto attachments, ideologies, or societal conditioning that impose their energies upon us. These influences persist as shadows throughout our lives, until we acknowledge and illuminate them or until we learn to coexist with them, always aware that they impede our journey toward our authentic, pure, and elevated selves. We can begin to heal and transform these aspects of ourselves, if they are not rooted in love, as we uncover these barriers, whether they manifest as inner shadows, internal roadblocks, or obstructions that cloud our judgments and decisions. We release what no longer aligns with the vibrational frequency of love, clearing away outdated belief systems and ingrained behaviors. Simultaneously, we learn to forgive ourselves for the actions or choices we have made along the way. This process is commonly referred to as shadow work, and it is through forgiveness that we unlock the door to our true potential. True forgiveness emanates from a place of genuine love and acceptance. When we receive the gift of true self-love, we extend forgiveness first to ourselves and then to others as well. This forgiveness sets off a chain reaction, propelling our growth and expansion.

As long as forgiveness remains at the core of our being, we will continue to evolve and develop, regardless of any pain, darkness, or weight we may encounter. We can forgive those who unknowingly caused harm, as we were once unaware ourselves. When we become conscious of our behaviors and make the conscious decision to change them, that is when enlightenment occurs. It is through this profound transformation that we are able to bring about lasting change and personal growth.

Contemplate what happens when we find ourselves trapped in a repetitive pattern or cycle, or are unable to break free from a victim mindset. These experiences are quite common, persisting until we grasp the associated lesson. Engaging in the challenging process of shadow work can be emotionally demanding, causing many individuals to struggle, as facing these shadows may not align with their planetary influences. This is precisely why our astrological birth charts hold such significance in guiding our conscious actions, beliefs, and thoughts. By examining the planetary positions during our birth and reflecting upon our life experiences through the lens of the zodiac wheel, we can identify repetitive patterns that require our attention for transformation. It is through recognizing these patterns that we begin to realize the necessity for change.

Embracing unity within all aspects of existence can be challenging for many, as they often perceive their own way as the only pathway. It can be difficult for them to grasp that life encompasses diverse expressions and that the collective whole is composed of its interconnected parts. The shadow aspects of ourselves are commonly associated with the ego, as they originate from our individual perspectives, the *I* mentality. However, embracing a holistic perspective allows us to acknowledge the presence of ego within us while also developing a broader understanding of humanity as a whole. This broader perspective opens the door to exploring solutions and engaging in a collaborative approach, moving beyond single-minded perceptions and limitations. By transcending the narrow confines of the ego, we gain the ability to recognize the collective complexities of humanity and work toward solutions that benefit all.

A life filled with blessings, but that has lacked experiences for growth, can be seen as one aspect within the broader perspective of the whole. While it may seem appealing on the surface, this scenario misses the valuable lessons and transformative experiences that come through challenges and personal growth from finding your light from within the dark. It is important to recognize and embrace the existence of this side, as it contributes to the complexity and diversity of life's tapestry. By acknowledging the different facets of existence, we cultivate a more holistic view that appreciates the interplay between blessings, hardships, and growth, recognizing that they all have their unique roles in our personal and collective journeys. A life characterized by high vibrations can indeed be seen as a privileged and blessed life, yet it may lack the broader perspective gained through overcoming obstacles and experiencing growth from diverse life circumstances. Individuals who have faced hardships and transformed their lives to embrace beauty and then go on to receive wealth and abundance possess a more expansive viewpoint and worldview. Their journey encompasses both the struggles and blessings, providing them with deep knowledge and understanding. Their vibrations resonate on a larger scale, reflecting the profound depth of their experiences and the wisdom that they have acquired. Embracing a wider-ranging perspective enriches their energetic presence and allows for a more profound connection to the collective energy of the world.

In the grand tapestry of our lives, every single experience, especially those that are difficult or burdensome, serves a purpose in our personal growth and development. It is important to remind ourselves that everything we face, no matter how challenging or distressing, is an opportunity for us to change, expand, and evolve our consciousness. Each obstacle we encounter possesses this potential to shape the trajectory of our lives, and every roadblock we face serves as a profound life lesson from which we can gain wisdom and insight. Even the most stressful days are filled with valuable lessons for us to acknowledge, learn from, and ultimately grow from.

The path of personal growth is not without its difficulties. We must be willing to confront the hardships head on, acknowledging the emotional toll they may have on us. In order to embark on this journey of repairing and transforming our very DNA, it is crucial to allow ourselves to feel deeply. By delving into the depths of our emotions, we enable ourselves to engage in the work of shadow exploration and healing from our most authentic and vulnerable place. It is through this process that we initiate a literal reprogramming of our DNA, realigning it with our true essence and unlocking our untapped potential. Shadow work, in essence, becomes the gateway to a profound transformation of our being. By consciously delving into the depths of our subconscious, we bring to light the suppressed aspects of ourselves that have held us back and hindered our progress. This intricate and introspective process involves peeling back the layers of conditioning, belief systems, traumas, and societal imprints that have subtly shaped our lives. As we unravel these hidden layers, we gain a deeper understanding of ourselves and the patterns that govern our actions and decisions. Through this understanding, we are empowered to release what no longer serves us and cultivate a new narrative that aligns with our higher purpose and true potential.

Embracing shadow work entails recognizing that our DNA carries imprints of past experiences and emotions, both favorable and unfavorable, light and heavy. By allowing ourselves to fully experience and process the emotions associated with these imprints, we begin the process of energetic release and healing. This transformative journey reprograms the very fabric of our DNA, enabling us to shed old patterns, limiting beliefs, and energetic baggage that may have weighed us down. As we navigate the complexities of shadow work, it is crucial to approach it with self-compassion and patience, acknowledging that this process of reprogramming is intricate and takes time.

What are some of the shadows we may encounter on a daily basis that may hinder our progress? Judgment of others and measuring ourselves against them are prevalent shadows that many individuals struggle with daily. Sexism, classism, and racism also serve as divisive tools that segregate humanity and facilitate judgment based on those categories. However, it is fear that is by far the greatest hindrance for all mankind, and the biggest tool used in controlling humans. Let's take a look at what types of shadows come up with fear.

- Fear: Fear of failure, judgment, or uncertainty can hold us back from taking risks and exploring new opportunities for growth.

- Self-Doubt: Negative self-talk and a lack of confidence can prevent us from fully embracing our potential or pursuing our goals.

- Comfort Zone: Staying within our comfort zone can limit our growth. It is important to push ourselves beyond familiar boundaries and embrace the discomfort that comes with personal evolution.

- Procrastination: Putting off tasks or delaying action can impede progress and prevent us from achieving our goals.

- Negative self-beliefs: Deeply rooted beliefs about ourselves, such as feeling unworthy or incapable, can hinder our progress and prevent us from reaching our full potential.

- Lack of self-discipline: A lack of consistency and discipline in our actions can hinder progress and make it difficult to develop new habits or skills.

- Resistance to change: Resisting change and clinging to our old patterns or ways of thinking can hinder personal development and limit our ability to adapt and evolve.

- Perfectionism: Striving for perfection can create immense pressure and lead to a fear of making mistakes, which can prevent us from trying new things and learning from experiences.

- Lack of accountability: Not taking responsibility for our actions and choices can hinder progress and prevent us from learning from our mistakes.

- External influences: Surrounding ourselves with negative or unsupportive individuals can hinder our growth and negatively impact our self belief.

Fear can manifest in various ways. Fear often leads to avoidance behavior. We may avoid certain situations, tasks, or challenges because we are afraid of failure, rejections, or discomfort.

Fear can manifest as negative self-talk, where we constantly criticize ourselves, and doubt our abilities. We may engage in self-sabotaging thoughts like *I'm not good enough* or *I will never succeed*. Fear can have physical manifestations, such as rapid heartbeat, sweating, trembling, shortness of breath, or even panic attacks. These symptoms can range from subtle discomfort to intense psychological reactions.

Fear can also lead to a perfectionist mindset, where we strive for flawless performance in order to avoid criticism or failure. We may set impossibly high standards for ourselves, leading to stress and dissatisfaction. Fear often feeds self-limiting beliefs that hold us back from pursuing our goals or taking risks. We may believe that we are not capable, not deserving, or that failure is inevitable.

Fear can further result in excessive over thinking and worrying about potential unfavorable outcomes. This can consume our mental energy and prevent us from taking action or enjoying the present moment. Fear of rejection or disapproval can lead to people-pleasing behavior, where we prioritize the needs and opinions of others over our own. This can hinder authenticity and personal development.

Fear can also lead to constant comparison with others and feeling envious of their achievements or possessions. This comparison mindset can diminish our self-worth and prevents us from celebrating our own progress and accomplishments.

Fear can drive a need for control as a way to manage uncertainty and minimize potential risks. This need for control can manifest as micromanaging, being overly rigid, or resisting change, ultimately hindering our adaptability. Fear can cause defensiveness and an unwillingness to receive feedback or accept differing opinions. The fear of being criticized or judged can make us defensive, hindering open communication and learning. Fear can lead to self-sabotaging behavior, where we undermine our own success or happiness due to subconscious fears of the unknown, fear of failure, or fear of stepping outside of our comfort zone.

Fear can result in social withdrawal and avoidance of vulnerability. We may avoid deep connections or opening up to others due to the fear of rejection, judgment, or emotional pain. Finally, fear can limit our choices and keep us from taking risks or pursuing new opportunities. We may choose the safe and familiar path instead of exploring new possibilities due to the fear of the unknown or fear of failure.

Fear is a natural human emotion and can serve as a protective mechanism. However, it is essential to recognize when fear is hindering our growth, and then to take steps to face and overcome it, allowing us to embrace personal evolution and pursue our goals with courage and resilience.

What is the worst outcome that could result from addressing our issues? We might fail, and be forced to try again and again until we succeed. What is the best outcome that could result from addressing our issues? We will succeed. Therefore, there is really nothing to fear on this healing journey. Those who are on this path are actively working to overcome their issues, and the key is to keep trying until you confront those difficulties like manipulation, passive-aggressiveness, rigidity, perfectionism, low self-esteem, anger, and fear. Some people are very skilled at pretending to be happy, which is why you should not compare yourself to anyone else. There's a common phrase I dislike, "Fake it until you make it." I don't care for it because if you can't acknowledge what you are truly feeling and have to resort to faking it, that pretense becomes a part of your energetic signature. If you are merely pretending, you deny yourself the opportunity to experience your emotions in the moment. Embracing your authentic self and accepting that it's okay to not be okay holds immense power—you don't have to fake anything. The only way to overcome your feelings is to acknowledge them and allow them to flow through you. You must accept your feelings and take ownership of them without projecting them onto others.

Someone once told me she wanted to be just like me, and it made me distance myself from her at that time because she was willing to give away all her power. Wanting to be someone other than yourself doesn't benefit anyone. People may use that desire for their own advantage, but that's manipulation. Manipulation is a harmful tactic that people use to feel better, often at the expense of someone else, due to a lack of boundaries. When you recognize potential manipulation, it is crucial to establish stronger boundaries. Unfortunately, manipulation is a commonly used tactic among those who feel a deep sense of lack, as this becomes part of their energetic signature. Capitalism thrives on the manipulative mindset, which leads us to believe that it is acceptable to want to be someone other than our true selves, ultimately teaching us to relinquish our individuality. These are some of the societal norms and ingrained conditioned layers we must peel back to uncover our authentic selves, allowing us to love who we truly are and, in turn, express that love fearlessly to the world.

When we confront all these difficult issues head on, courageously peering across the dark abyss of the unknown void, we are literally facing our fears directly. It is through trust and surrender that we will find the guidance and strength to accomplish this. Trust and surrender encompass two facets: trust in oneself in order to trust and surrender with the universe. The manifestation of these two forms of trust varies individually in each person's life. Trust in oneself is characterized by several key aspects, including:

- Self-belief: Trusting in oneself involves having faith in your abilities, qualities, and judgments. It means recognizing and appreciating your strengths and having confidence in your decisions.

- Self-acceptance: Trust in yourself also involves accepting and embracing oneself fully—including both strengths and areas for growth, meaning acknowledging your flaws and imperfections without judgments or self criticism.

- Authenticity: Trusting yourself entails staying true to your values, beliefs, and desires. It means honoring your own authenticity and not compromising personal integrity for the sake of others' expectations.

- Listening to intuition: Trust in yourself is closely tied to listening to your intuition or inner wisdom. It means trusting those subtle gut feelings, instincts, or inner guidance that provide insights and direction.

- Resilience: Trust in yourself involves having the resilience to bounce back from setbacks or failures. It means believing in your ability to overcome obstacles, learn from challenges, and grow stronger through adversity.

- Taking risks: Trusting in yourself often means being open to taking calculated risks and stepping outside your comfort zone. It means having the confidence to pursue new opportunities, embrace uncertainty, and learn from both failures and successes.

- Honoring boundaries: Trusting in yourself includes setting and honoring personal boundaries. It means advocating for your needs, saying no when necessary, and establishing healthy limits in relationships and situations.

- Self-care: Trusting in yourself involves prioritizing self-care and nurturing your physical, emotional, and mental well-being. It means recognizing the importance of self-nourishment and allocating time for rest, relaxation, and activities that bring joy and fulfillment.

When you have trust and faith in yourself, you naturally develop trust and faith in the universe in order to surrender to its wisdom. Trust in the universe can be characterized by the following elements.

- Surrender to the flow: Trusting in the universe involves surrendering to the natural flow of life. It means accepting that there are larger forces at play, and having faith that things will unfold as they are meant to, even if it may not align with your initial expectations or desires.

- Letting go of control: Trust in the universe requires releasing the need for excessive control. It means allowing life to unfold organically, understanding that we cannot control every outcome, and having faith in the greater wisdom of the universe.

- Trust in the synchronicities and signs: Trusting in the universe involves recognizing and interpreting synchronicity's meaningful coincidences and signs that guide us along our path. It means being open to the signs and having faith that they are guiding us in the right direction.

- Gratitude and acceptance: Trusting in the universe includes cultivating gratitude for both the pleasant and the challenging experiences we encounter. It means accepting that every experience serves a purpose and contributes to our growth and evolution.

- Alignment with universal principles: Trust in the universe involves aligning ourselves with the universal principles such as love, compassion, and interconnectedness. It means recognizing that we are each part of a greater whole and trusting in the inherent goodness and wisdom of the universe.

- Patience and divine timing: Trust in the universe requires cultivating patience and understanding that things may unfold in their own divine timing. It means refraining from forcing outcomes and trusting that what is meant for us will manifest at the right time.

- Positive outlook: Trusting in the universe involves maintaining a positive outlook and having assurance that the universe is on our side. It means reframing challenges as opportunities for growth and viewing setbacks as steppingstones toward our desired outcomes.

It is important to note that trust in the universe is deeply personal and can take different forms for each individual. It is a practice of cultivating certainty and confidence in the interconnectedness of all things and trusting in the inherent wisdom and guidance in both the universe and yourself. With such varied lifestyles in the world, it can be challenging to perceive the broader perspective and find the positive aspects within our struggles. This is why it is crucial to overcome the limitations of the ego mindset. By recognizing that our challenges are opportunities for personal growth, we can transcend stress into valuable lessons learned. This shift allows us to reframe our thoughts, accept circumstances differently, and view events as not happening TO us but FOR us.

Here are a variety of basic tools and techniques that can be used for shadow work in your life right now, and that all have a long history with humans. If you are actively engaged with working on the mind–body–spirit connection, doing chakra work, practicing yoga, and meditating, you are already doing shadow work simply by engaging in the introspective process.

- Self-reflection: Engaging in self-reflection, by journaling, contemplating, or introspective processing, allows you to explore your thoughts, emotions, and patterns of behavior. It helps uncover underlying beliefs and fears that may be a part of your shadow.

- Yoga: Yoga serves as more than just physical exercise; it's a pathway to delve deep into your psyche, confronting the shadows lurking within. Through mindful movement and pranayama, practitioners peel back layers of the self, exploring and integrating aspects often buried beneath the surface. This journey of introspection and shadow work in yoga fosters self-awareness, acceptance, and, ultimately, personal growth.

- Meditation and mindfulness: Practicing meditation and mindfulness can help you develop awareness of your thoughts, emotions, and sensations. By observing them without judgment, you can identify patterns and unconscious aspects of yourself.

- Inner child work: This involves connecting with and healing your inner child, who may hold unresolved emotions and traumas. Through activities like visualization dialogue or creative expression, you can nurture and heal this aspect of yourself.

- Dream analysis: Paying attention to your dreams and analyzing their symbolism can provide insight into your unconscious mind and aspects of your shadow.

- Emotional awareness and expression: Actively acknowledging and allowing yourself to feel and express a wide range of emotions is an important part of shadow work. This helps bring subconscious aspects to the surface for examination and integration.

- Therapy and counseling: Working with a qualified therapist or counselor can provide guidance, support, and a safe space for exploring your shadow. They can help uncover deeper patterns and provide tools for healing and integration.

- Shadow journaling: Keeping a dedicated journal specifically for shadow work allows you to record and reflect upon experiences, insights, and observations related to your shadows. It helps track progress and identify recurring themes or patterns.

- Shadow integration exercises: Engaging in specific exercises or rituals designed for shadow integration, such as visualization, dialogue with aspects of your shadow, or symbolic representation, can aid in the process of integrating shadow aspects into your conscious awareness.

- Confronting triggers: Identify specific situations or people that trigger strong emotional reactions in you. When you experience a trigger, take a moment to reflect on what emotions come up and why. Try asking yourself questions on what these emotions say about yourself or what you might be trying to avoid. Instead of reacting immediately, try exploring these emotions to find out the underlying reasons these feelings and opinions arise within you.

Shadow work is deeply personal and different tools may resonate with different individuals. It is important to find what works best for you and approach shadow work with patience, self-compassion, and a willingness to explore in order to heal.

In my present life, I find peace and fulfillment as I embrace the relaxation and enjoyment that comes with my later years and the wisdom gained through my experiences. Despite having done extensive inner work, I continuously embark on the journey of shadow work, approaching it with a fresh perspective each time. One way I engage in this process is by reflecting upon what activities or pursuits bring me the greatest joy. As my sources of joy may vary from day to day, the question remains constant, while my answers and the resulting outcomes continue to evolve. Creating in any form brings me the greatest joy. Whether it's making holistic wellness teas for my body, crafting incense to enhance my mental projections during sacred rituals, or blending aromatherapy oils for meditation with my spirit, I find immense satisfaction in these creative expressions. I just need to listen to my body, mind, and spirit to find out what it needs!

I also find tremendous joy in writing and producing music. This favorite activity allows me to merge magical words with enchanting sounds and vibrations, creating a unique blend of personal expression. It is through this musical process that I am able to release and let go fully, embracing the best version of myself. Music serves as a powerful tool for my evolution, and I strive to leverage its potential to my advantage in this realm of personal growth and expression.

Music serves as a bridge that transcends human culture, races, and languages. It encompasses both the enchantment of spells and the power of sounds and vibrations. When I engage in the act of making music, I enter into a state of pure bliss, fully present in the now. This elevated vibrational state naturally aligns with the essence of meditation. I delight in becoming entranced, allowing myself to journey into a meditative state. This practice harnesses the profound power of the shaman, and it is accessible to all of us at no cost. We all possess the ability to utilize music for free as a potent tool for personal transformation and spiritual exploration.

As we understand the true power of music, not just in its lyrics—which are words that create spells—but also in the energy that it carries when we create or enjoy it, we can begin to discern what music ought to be for us, aiding in our personal and spiritual development. Are we consuming content that disrespects women? Are we engaging with material that hinders our advancement? Are we replacing our moments of silence with music that diminishes the human experience, or are we committed to championing artists who strive to uplift humanity? What is our emotional state after listening to music we enjoy? What specifically did we appreciate about the music? If the content was hateful or degrading, and yet we found pleasure in it, can we recognize how this diminishes our human experience and our connections with each other? Can we acknowledge how this affects our sense of responsibility and accountability with each other?

"Hate begets hate, and violence begets violence"—Martin Luther King Jr.

Certainly our emotional state is often reflected in the music we create or enjoy. In times of sadness, we are drawn to melancholic music, while in moments of joy we gravitate toward uplifting, cheerful music. Music serves as a direct reflection of our state of mind.

In Chapter 4, we look into the profound concepts of karma and the universal laws. This discussion is of great significance, as many individuals experience a series of events that may seem inexplicable, leaving them yearning for deeper understanding and clarity in their lives. It is essential to acknowledge that these discussions carry weighted energy, and not everyone may feel compelled to engage with them. However, those who resonate within the alignment of their birth charts and their life-path callings will find resonance and answers to difficult life experiences in these explorations. When you establish a state of balance within yourself and synchronize with the laws and the principles of the universe, a harmonious existence unfolds. When your body, mind, and spirit align, synchronicities begin to manifest in your life as you follow through on the principles and trust in the guidance of the universe.

However, even when we embrace these practices, challenges still arise. These challenges serve as valuable lessons that are rooted in the very purpose of our soul's journey and the growth we are here to experience. By continuously learning and growing, we invite further lessons into our lives. Our bodies and minds are not meant to become stagnant within this time-frame. Instead, we are encouraged to seize the opportunity for growth and evolution while we are present on this planet. Facing our fears becomes pivotal on this journey, as it allows us to dance harmoniously with our vibrational essence in the vast cosmos, engaging with all that surrounds us. Through this self-actualization and interaction, we unlock our fullest potential.

Can you imagine a world full of self-actualized humans? If we collectively imagine a world where all individuals are self-actualized, perhaps this transformation will occur more rapidly, driven by the prevailing energies that surround us. The dawning of the Aquarian Era signals this shift toward a reality where self-actualization becomes more prevalent.

Below are some questions to ask yourself when embarking on inner shadow work toward self-actualization.

- What are the aspects of myself that I habitually hide or suppress from others, and even myself?

- How do past experiences or traumas influence my current beliefs, behaviors, and perceptions?

- What reoccurring patterns or emotions trigger discomfort or resistance within me?

- In what ways do I project my fears, insecurities, or unresolved issues onto others?

- How can I cultivate self-compassion and acceptance toward the less desirable parts of myself as I strive for growth and authenticity?

- What fears or limiting beliefs hold me back from fully embracing my true self and expressing myself authentically?

- How do societal norms, family expectations, or cultural influences shape my self-perception and behaviors?

- What role does self-forgiveness play in releasing past guilt, shame, or regret that may be inhibiting my personal growth?

- How do I integrate the emotions and traits within me that I find challenging or uncomfortable?

- In what ways can I cultivate a deeper connection with my intuition and inner wisdom to guide me on my path of self-discovery and healing?

CHAPTER 4:
Lessons From Karma- And The Universal Laws

I feel that karma, and the Universal Laws are an integral part of this book and to the ladder of self-actualization. Although not all will be inclined to go deeply into these subjects, the inclusion of the universal laws and karma in this book stems from the wealth of profound information they have offered me. As I embarked on my healing journey, I began to uncover and experience these universal laws, which were, remarkably, reflecting in my own life. It became clear to me that the teachings of these laws seamlessly aligned with my personal experiences and provided a comprehensive framework for understanding the dynamics of existence. The ease with which I could perceive the connection between these laws in my own life further validated their significance to the knowledge they imparted.

The twelve universal laws are thought to be timeless principles that ancient cultures uncovered through observation. Some link these laws to Hawaiian meditations, while others trace their origins to ancient Egyptian philosophy and to scientifically observable data. Sir Isaac Newton was considered to be one discoverer of the universal laws, but even he recognized that his success was built on the backs those before him like Galileo and Johannes Kepler. Galileo was condemned by the church and treated terribly toward the end of his life, however, we honor his name in science and astronomy today. This goes to show you that those who are expanding their conscious awareness are not always received well, considering they aren't going with the norm but challenging it. These men held many titles and aspirations, but one thing they all had in common was their love of science. They were using a higher capacity in their conscious awareness, and they were still only utilizing a small fraction of their true capacity. This is a stark reminder to all of us to look at all the room we still have in our awareness for growth and expansion.

I do have to highlight that the concept of the twelve universal laws is not universally accepted or recognized within all spiritual or philosophical traditions. My purpose here is not to simply adhere to universally accepted spiritual or philosophical traditions. Instead, I am here to absorb knowledge, question existing norms, and potentially modify or combine them, as well as to share these insights with others.

Below are the twelve laws that are generally attributed to the universal laws in certain belief systems.

1. Law of Divine Oneness: All things are interconnected and part of a divine whole.

2. Law of Vibration: Everything in the universe is in a constant state of motion, creating vibrations of different frequencies.

3. Law of Correspondences: As above, so below. The patterns and dynamics observed in the universe are reflected on all levels of existence.

4. Law of Cause and Effect: Every action has a corresponding reaction or outcome.

5. Law of Attraction: Like attracts like. Our thoughts, beliefs, and emotions attract corresponding experiences in some way.

6. Law of Perpetual Transmutation of Energy: Energy is constantly transforming from one form to another.

7. Law of Relativity: Everything is relative and can only be understood in equivalence to something else.

8. Law of Polarity: Everything has polar opposites or complimentary forces.

9. Law of Rhythm: Everything moves in cycles, with ups and downs, expansions, and contractions.

10. Law of Gender: Everything in the universe has masculine and feminine energies, creating balance and harmony.

11. Law of Non-Resistance: When we resist a condition, person, or thing that we don't like or want, we are literally giving power to it. Resistance to what causes suffering hinders growth. Acceptance and surrender to the flow leads to harmony in life.

12. Law of Mentalism: All is the mind. The universe is mental in nature, and our thoughts create our reality.

It is important to note that these laws may be interpreted and understood differently across various belief systems and traditions. Some sources may combine these laws or present them in different ways. It is up to the individual to explore these laws and discern what laws resonate with their own spiritual beliefs and experiences. There are countless resources available on these universal laws, much of which can be obtained for free on the Internet. Whether these universal laws are accepted universally, they are still fundamentally centered around embracing unity and embodying your life through love and interconnectedness.

Embodying the universal laws and applying them in our lives is a journey that brings about a deeper sense of alignment and fulfillment. Living in harmony with these principles allows us to create a life that reflects our highest potential and brings forth love, joy, and abundance. Embracing these laws can help us climb the ladder of a successful venture to our highest selves, which is love and connection to a higher plane or dimension of consciousness.

Karma is a tool that helps maintain balance and harmony within the cycles of our various lives. Karma can be both favorable and unfavorable, depending on what needs to be balanced in life. It is shaped by the principle of cause and effect and, depending on the lessons we are able to learn from our experiences, will depend on the influences in the future.

Every person on Earth is intertwined with karma. All the wonderful things in your life are the result of your karma, just as the challenges you face are also a part of it. Many people tend to view karma solely in an unfavorable fashion, but this is only half of karma's energetic signature. From the moment of my birth, my life was entangled with karma, and I found myself perpetually trapped in a victim mentality. Despite my constant efforts to improve, grow, and confront my problems, I often succumbed to emotions before seeking understanding. However, everything changed after my contact experience in 2020, as I received a transformative gift that liberated me from all my sources of suffering. This was precisely what I had asked for during my meditation, albeit on a much grander scale than I had anticipated. Now, reflecting on my past traumas no longer serves me. Although I learned valuable lessons from each experience, I have relinquished the victim mindset and embrace a present-focused mindset. My life is now centered on what is actually unfolding in the here and now. The past, with all its trials and tribulations, has served its purpose and provided me with the challenges I could handle, as well as balanced my soul's karma. Even the people I was attracted to brought in the opposite energy. If my life was dedicated to the pursuit of truth, I was receiving people with secrets and hidden agendas, or with hidden aspects of themselves. This explains why I encountered numerous lessons along the way, as I was genuinely committed to doing the necessary work for a better life.

Family karma refers to the karmic patterns, challenges, and imbalances that are inherited and shared among family members through generations. It suggests that unresolved issues, karmic debt, and unresolved emotions can perpetuate and manifest within family dynamics. Family karma operates on the principle that the actions and consequences of previous generations can impact the experiences and circumstances of current and future family members. It can manifest in various ways, including repeated relationship patterns, religious or spiritual matters, health issues, financial challenges, or reoccurring emotional behavior patterns within the family. The concept of family karma recognizes that individuals are born into families not only to share love and support but also to learn and resolve karmic lessons. It suggests that specific souls may choose to reincarnate into a particular family to work through specific karmic imbalances or dynamics. The karmic trench, also known as generational karmic patterns, refers to deeply ingrained karmic imbalances or challenging behavior patterns that span multiple generations. It represents a collective karmic challenge that needs resolution, often manifesting as a long-standing issue or patterns within a family's lineage. The karmic trench can be seen as a metaphorical trench or groove that family members find themselves repeating, perpetuating certain behaviors or challenges. This could include patterns of addiction, abuse, cyclical relationship issues, financial hardships, or other recurring difficulties.

Breaking free from the karmic trench requires awareness, healing, and conscious choices. By recognizing and acknowledging these patterns, family members can actively work to resolve and transform these karmic imbalances. This may involve deep inner work, forgiveness, healing past traumas, or seeking professional guidance when needed. Addressing family karma often involves healing not only the individual but also healing the collective energy of the family lineage. Through this process, individuals can break free from the confines of the karmic patterns, release unfavorable energies, and create a new cycle of healing and growth within the family. It is important to note that while family karma in the karmic trench can be influential in shaping our experiences and relationships, it does not determine our destiny or limit our potential for personal growth.

By bringing awareness to these patterns and actively working toward healing and transformation, individuals can pave the way for practical change, liberation, and the realization of their true potential. Understanding the family karmic trench can provide valuable insights into the dynamics and challenges within the family system. It encourages individuals to develop compassion, forgiveness, and mindfulness in their interactions with family members, offering an opportunity for personal and collective healing. Remember to respect all members of the family in this type of dynamic. Sometimes you will find that individuals do not want to heal themselves or their family, or get rid of the victim mindset, because it is the only place they are comfortable living. This is where boundaries come in handy, so that you are comfortable doing your work while not letting others hinder your progress. You can do the work even if your family isn't willing to do the same. Do not allow the mindset of others to block you from achieving your goals.

Family karma does not necessarily indicate wrongdoing within a family or a need for atonement. Understanding the intricate balance of life throughout our soul's journey reveals that we purposefully seek knowledge from all facets of existence. Remember, if we are entrapped in challenges, we chose this path, believing in our ability to navigate it—to restore balance from past lives before our present earthly incarnation. We make conscious choices, aware of the challenges and experiences awaiting us. We embrace these hardships as we acknowledge that we have the strength to carry them, recognizing the necessity for life's anchoring side. Life is made up of both heavy and lighter burdens, and if we have lived easier lives before we willingly select challenging paths to grow from in this life. Every individual bravely fulfills their unique Dharma by simply existing here. Every single person is living their dharma, no matter what path they are on currently, and all lives here have an energetic frequency contributing to the grand cosmic scale of life's existence as it is for us today.

Balance is how we are able to exist here, so both sides of the spectrum are needed. The diverse experiences collectively woven propel us forward on our evolutionary journey. Progress toward higher consciousness is not a sudden leap but a gradual climb, like ascending a ladder. Though some steps may seem lost to time, our steady progression reflects the continual ascent of humanity, step-by-step, toward finding our light source. Throughout history, countless individuals have discovered their inner light, not just those immortalized in written accounts. However, some become so enamored with this light that they simply gaze upon it, much like an eye atop of the pyramid. After climbing to the pinnacle and facing the light, one can choose to simply turn around. Turning around signifies a shift; one is no longer at the peak but overlooking everything; one that holds, binds, and influences all below. The key lies in understanding what comes next, what to do after discovering your light. It is about the journey forward. Many may have already found their light, especially in this era of the rapid expansion of consciousness. Yet, not everyone knows what comes next. The next step is to turn around, to merge with the unified whole, and actively participate in supporting and sustaining the interconnected web of existence. As you hold space for others to ascend, when your role ends you will re-enter the cycle, rebalancing and contributing from a different vantage point to maintain the harmony of the system. I call this system the Great Engine, as it was revealed to me in the data download during my contact experience.

The origin story of my personal family karma traces back to a few lives; some lived thousands of years ago and some lived in the last century, although I am uncertain of the exact time frame. These were revelations I had at different times. One of these revelations came after a teacher prompted me to dive into the exploration of my Akashic records, also known as the "Book of Life"; a topic that will be covered in the next chapter. This teacher labeled me as an evil queen in Egypt in one of my past lives, and stated that my current life was influenced by karmic lessons from that life. Driven by a desire to understand the reasons behind my karmic experiences and to check the accuracy of her claim, I embarked on a journey within. Through meditation and establishing a connection with my higher self, I sought answers to those inquiries. Trusting in the guidance of my higher self, I knew the answers would come. In order to comprehend all of my family's karma via the Akashic records, I required a comprehensive holistic viewpoint.

Presently, my life consists mainly of Yin energetic vibrations and connections with Goddess or Divine Feminine energy. I carry two mother wounds within my natal birth chart. The moon is set at the apex of two planetary triangles, a configuration known as the Finger of Fate, or Finger of God. These alignments, with the moon as the apex planet, signify the presence of the mother wound within my astrological chart. This is reflected not only in my profound bond with Mother Earth but also in the patterns of separation and detachment associated with my own biological mother. As I started exploring the origins of my own energetic abilities, I began to investigate the natal charts of others, seeking insights into how they found their light and shared it with the world, much like Buddha and Yeshua. Through this exploration, I discovered that Yeshua carried profound connection to Divine Masculine Energy, often associated with the Father Consciousness. Additionally, the presence of the grand cross in his chart symbolized a collective burden.

By examining astrological references and prominent narratives, we can gain a deeper understanding of the energies and expressions of historical figures, bridging the gap between ancient wisdom and observable phenomenon in nature, as well as the enduring stories and mythos that shape the legacies of those who will follow in their footsteps. Guided by my intuition, I was led to a male teacher, well versed in the traditions of the Kabbalah in Jewish mysticism. This path, which had predominantly been associated with male practitioners, was something entirely new and unfamiliar to me. It had not previously piqued my interest, but I recognized its potential to offer the knowledge and understanding I sought. I was in a state of profound connection when I received these insights, which I will discuss in the next chapter.

On our healing and spiritual journeys, surrendering and trusting in the universe and its process play pivotal roles. As you witness progress and experience the manifestation of your desires, your belief in your abilities strengthens, heightening awareness of your potential to achieve your goals. The state of being fully present holds tremendous value, as it is within this activated state of awareness that we accomplish our most significant goals. By letting go of attachments and surrendering to what serves our highest good, we open up to the flow of divine guidance and allow the universe to support our journey of growth and fulfillment.

When exploring the universal laws and the impact they have on your life, consider asking yourself the following questions.

- How does the law of attraction manifest in my experiences and the outcomes that I attract into my life?

- In what ways do I align with the law of cause and effect, recognizing the repercussions of my actions and decisions?

- How can I harmonize with the law of vibration to raise my energetic frequency and attract better experiences into my life that coincide with my authentic desires?

- How do the planetary placements in my natal chart align with universal laws, such as the law of attraction or karma, and how can this awareness enhance my self-discovery and personal growth?

- In what ways can I leverage the insights from my astrological chart to work in harmony with the universal laws, such as the law of polarity or law of correspondence, in my life?

- How can the integration of astrological knowledge and the universal laws empower me to navigate challenges, embrace opportunities, and co-create a life that resonates with my authentic self and higher purpose?

- How do the energies indicated in my natal chart, such as YOD formations or the grand cross, align with the universal laws, and what lessons or growth opportunities do they present for my spiritual journey and personal development?

- How can I work with the insights provided by my natal chart and an understanding of the universal laws to transmute and release any heavy energies or burdens, thereby fostering healing, inner peace, and alignment with my higher purpose and spiritual evolution?

- How can I align the patterns and energies revealed in my natal chart with the principles of the universal laws to create a harmonious and fulfilling life experience that nurtures my happiness and well-being?

- In what ways can I leverage my knowledge of astrological influences and universal laws to cultivate a mindset of gratitude, abundance, and self empowerment, leading to a deeper sense of joy, purpose, and contentment in my daily life?

CHAPTER 5:

Why Are You Here? Akashic Records and Finding Your True Path

In the realm of the Akashic records, there exists an abundance of websites, individuals, and locales that offer access to these sacred archives. However, I assure you that the most profound revelations and insights come from establishing a personal connection with your own higher self and embarking on that journey yourself. I will share a list of books for further recommended reading on the subject for those interested in deepening their self-study on how to access the Akashic records in the back of this book. In fact, I will provide a list of books that have supported me on my journey, should you wish to explore any of these avenues further. However, feel free to follow whatever resonates with your energy. There is a plethora of information out there regarding the knowledge I have shared in this book, which I gained through life experience along my journey.

It is through this personal exploration that you will discover the answers you seek far more effectively than relying solely on external sources. I speak from first-hand experience, as I, too, discovered that the true power lies within your own connection to your higher self. When I set forth on this path, it became evident that the wisdom and knowledge obtained through my personal journey surpassed what others could provide. Trusting in your own capacity to explore the depths of the Akashic records will unearth precise understanding and revelations that are meant just for you.

The Akashic records hold immense significance as a vast databank of information that transcends space and time. They contain the collective knowledge, emotions, and experiences of every soul throughout history. Accessing the Akashic records can provide deep insight, profound healing, and a greater understanding of one's life purpose. By tapping into this infinite well of wisdom, individuals can gain clarity, find guidance, and unlock their full potential, offering a transformative opportunity for personal growth and spiritual evolution.

Often referred to as the Book of Life, navigating the Akashic records can be a time-consuming process that requires discernment regarding when to utilize this powerful tool. When I initially visited my Akashic records, I gained limited insight into my life from another person's perspective. Years later, however, during my own exploration of the records, I received insightful revelations regarding the underlying reasons for the karmic life I am living today. It was a challenge for me to comprehend that certain aspects of our current experiences may be linked to energies from past lifetimes, where we are paying for or working through specific karmic lessons or debts. Such realizations highlight the intricacies of our spiritual journey and emphasize the significance of carefully diving into the depths of the Akashic records with respect and understanding. The awareness that I have come to acquire about karma, our past lives, and their energy signatures is slightly different than what was taught to me in the past. This was something revealed to me after my contact experience, related to this life and its true purpose.

***Before proceeding, I feel it is important to give a fair warning. The forthcoming discussion will dive into topics from previous lives that may contain graphic and undesirable elements. I kindly request you to reserve judgment, as these experiences do not pertain to my current existence but rather represent a connection of soul and spirit that I am actively balancing in this* *lifetime. It has taken me considerable time and effort to process and come to terms with this information, let alone be able to be this vulnerable and open about myself with everyone. That in itself is a great feat. This is vulnerable authenticity.*

Caution: The following content encompasses heavy and heartfelt personal energies derived from past life regression insights, retrieved from my Akashic records.

As I delved into the profound realm of the Akashic records, I had already journeyed through several decades of life, accumulating a wealth of experiences along the way. Having cultivated an abundance mindset and lifestyle, and embracing the ebb and flow of life, I found myself comfortable with my own being. I was content to receive the blessings of this existence after all the work I had already done and just simply be. However, the synchronicities of life continued to persistently beckon for my attention. The signs led me toward encounters with numerous teachers, each playing a significant role on my spiritual journey.

One particular teacher stands out, the one who shocked me by expelling me from their group for speaking my truth about altruism in spirituality. This is what the entire group was instructed to do: speak your truth. I felt compelled to speak my truth due to the experiences I had received in the group's guided meditation. I encountered an apparition of Buddha within a golden Sri Yantra before me, but I wasn't a Buddhist. I was experiencing the fifth dimension in my higher-self state for the first time that I was consciously aware of. The feelings and emotions I was tapped into during the meditation allowed for a state of bliss, and I instantly wanted to share it with everyone. The teacher removed me from the group instead of engaging in dialogue simply because I expressed my truth, which contradicted her principles for running her business.

My truth centered around altruism in spirituality, which clearly didn't align with her beliefs, yet she showed no interest in discussing it with me. I had invested a significant amount of money in this group because I wanted to share the experience with my friends to aid in their personal journeys. When I inquired about what had occurred, my best friend sent me a screenshot of the teacher's response to the group. The teacher had informed everyone that I was living a life dictated by karma, stating that the only reason I felt compelled to do these good things for free for others was because I had been an evil queen of Egypt in a past life, and I was seeking redemption in this one. I felt as though she had twisted and distorted the magical experiences I had shared with her and her group about my trip to Egypt, reinterpreting them in a hurtful manner. This ordeal was deeply painful at the time, prompting me to seek solitude as I attempted to uncover the lessons meant for me in that experience. This took place during the first quarter of 2017, and following this incident I removed myself from the Internet, deleting all social media outlets that I had been a part of.

When I realized how much money I had spent, and knowing that most others could not afford such high prices, I was prompted to envision ways to help others without asking for money. If I encountered states of bliss in meditation and was having third eye visions after altruistic spiritual thinking, then anyone could. How was I the only one not wanting monetary gain for spiritual endeavors? I believed that truly considering someone my sister meant freely sharing my knowledge with them. I grappled with the paradox of being guided to an energy that was profoundly loving, yet facing resentment for expressing it. This led to two years of intense internal introspection.

Essentially, the apparition of Buddha told me that I carry Tara energy. So, I devoted those two years to acquainting myself with her, discovering her significance as a female Buddha; in some areas of the world, she is considered the mother to all bodhisattva. The entire interaction sparked my inner curiosity, prompting me to dive into the exploration of my past life karma. Like assembling the pieces of a puzzle, I received this information as I progressed through my journey. Every meditation session unveiled a new truth, like climbing a ladder of my mental awareness. Initially I had dismissed her allegations of my karmic ties to being an evil queen of Egypt.

Now, I was becoming aware of certain truths behind those allegations. I pondered whether my devotion to the Divine Mother, who symbolizes the dark, necessitated a shift in perspective. Perhaps I needed to seek insight from Great Father. Maybe I needed some Yang Divine Masculine energy to balance my mind and balance my life in order to receive these insights.

It was during this time that I found the male teacher, a practitioner of Kabbalah. Instantly, a profound connection was felt, as this teacher, too, had experienced the intricacies of a heavy karmic life. Under his guidance, I dived into the exploration of various evocations, including those of light angels and Kabbalist methods for protection. While these practices expanded my understanding of various spiritual realms and offered tools for magical spell casting, I yearned for deeper answers. Spell casting hadn't satisfied my quest in years. I had already manifested my dream life, but I sought profound knowledge and clarity.

I turned to meditation again, as this is the practice I had already embraced for years and had already connected deeply with myself there. I knew the only way to get what you want is to ask for it. After engaging in a ritual of protection, I called upon Yeshua, seeking his assistance in acquiring the knowledge I yearned for. I wanted to understand those allegations and comprehend the intricate balancing energies that had burdened me for more than four decades. The weight of heavy karma had become exhausting, and I sought to comprehend the nature of this cosmic counterbalance on a profound level.

Through my well-established connection with the divine via my higher-self light consciousness, I invoked the support of Yeshua to guide me on this quest for understanding. As this was a new aspect and area for me, I didn't know what to anticipate. Numerous questions arose within me, but what I did know—I felt deserving. I felt as though I had put in the effort, despite my past experiences. If there was mother energy then there was also father energy, and I knew I could communicate with him just as I did with her.

In a profound moment, I only had to think of asking with words, however no verbal communication was actually used at all. Instead, an overwhelming dominant energy transported me into the consciousness of a woman—literally pushing me inside her consciousness—allowing me to intimately experience her emotions and understand her feelings while seeing through her eyes. Within this understanding, a realization emerged alongside an acute awareness of her actions. I became aware that I was, indeed, mentally perceiving that I was reliving my Solar life, assuming the role of a queen in ancient Egypt. Contrary to what I was told, I was not inherently evil, although I did engage in unfavorable deeds.

In this past life, circumstances compelled me to commit one of the most heinous acts imaginable: the murder of my own family, followed by usurping control of the kingdom. The arduous truth that I came to comprehend was this: My beauty was revered by the entire kingdom. Admiration arose because my family had engaged in centuries of incestuous practices, resulting in deformities among them. The acts they perpetrated upon one another exacerbated these genetic deformities. My birth, however, was different. I was not a product of the same incestuous actions, but rather born from my mother's love for someone else. My father—the king—knew that I was not his daughter, but I was still of his blood since my mother was his sister. He loved me more than any of my other siblings.

This is how I gained the love of others, because of my father's favor. It was my physical beauty that gave me the ability to take on these roles. It was my destiny to assume this role and initiate a transformative shift within that kingdom. In order to alter the paradigm and break free from the cycles of incest, I felt compelled to undertake this difficult action. I don't know the name or exact identity of this woman, but her emotions were not those of an inherently evil individual—a limited, dualistic mindset of someone not yet ready to understand the true polarity of energies. This woman grappled with overwhelming guilt and remorse, but harbored a profound sense of hope for a different life. She wanted to escape the fate of being married to a deformed brother, perpetuating the lineage through incest.

Upon further insight, I was led to understand that humanity's evolution stagnated within that unbalanced system, prompting the need for an introduction of new energy, vitality, and a fresh paradigm. Thousands of years ago, an unbalanced matriarchal system, dictated by centuries of inbreeding defined life—a precursor to our contrasting yet similarly unbalanced patriarchal system today. Power and control is the narrative within unbalanced systems.

It is these complex circumstances that led to my abandonment by my family in this current life, carrying the weight of karma that I am now actively balancing. My experiences while visiting Egypt in this current life were deeply rooted in my connection to that past life, and to the land itself. This connection stemmed from the energetic imprints left behind, allowing me to recognize and reconnect with the familiar energetic signature of my light soul. It was through this resonance and alignment that I found myself drawn back to the sacred motherland and its profound history, unveiling a deeper understanding of my soul's journey across lifetimes.

After my extraterrestrial contact experience, I made several inquiries about this with them. They indulged me by allowing me to understand that I have a purpose in this life, just as I had a purpose in that life. Human life was not progressing nor evolving, and I came in to redirect energies and DNA. Ultimately, it was all about making sure DNA was evolving. Humans nowadays are at a similar standstill in evolution. Something has to change or trigger a change in order for humans to redirect evolution.

The extraterrestrials that are here with us have one job: monitoring our evolution. Sometimes you have to get rid of what was in order to make room for what will be. This is my life purpose: to hold space for what could be, to support the infinite, and to bring in the necessary energy for balancing this system. I live to achieve a purpose of helping humanity evolve, balance my soul's karma, and elevate and illuminate my soul's path.

Following that specific reading of my Akashic records, during my meditation I posed the question: Could I receive insights into what a balanced life for me looked like? I yearned to comprehend the cycles and rhythms of existence. If I were living my lunar life and it looks like the solstice of winter, filled with Yin energy, and my Egyptian life and experiences mirrored the sun's energies and exuded Yang energy, I craved understanding of my Equinox life—a life characterized by balance, especially after encountering the other heavy, dense, and intense energies. My understanding is that our life cycles mirror that of the patterns and cycles we see here on earth.

Remarkably, when I inquired about this I was informed that I already possess the answer within me. All I had to do was tap into my own inner wisdom to find the key. When I do that, it shows me that my passions and joys in this life are directly linked to that life. One such passion is Mongolian and Tuvan cultures, their music and throat singing, which has a profoundly soothing effect on my soul. Interestingly, my son possesses the ability to perform this art instinctively, without anyone teaching him except himself. Although he doesn't practice it often, he did so specifically for me, knowing how much I love it.

It is evident he has a natural connection to Mongolia, given his innate talents in this realm. I also have a deep reverence for Mongolia and its people. Now, I understand what a balanced life feels like when you are able to express yourself freely and creatively, and when your life is fulfilled. Music was everything to me in that life. I have an ear for it in this life, and I gave it to my son, just like my father had an ear for it and gave it to me. Playing any kind of music brings me great joy, but I didn't pursue it heavily in this life until recently. I am going to explore my ever-evolving creative side now that I can focus on something other than healing. Lately, though, it is mostly about writing lyrics.

Studying astrology alongside my studies of the Akashic records has provided me with an in-depth understanding of my planetary placements and their profound connection to my life's true path. I still work on it to this day because I have so many intricate details to meditate on and work through. I personally have two planets that rule my natal chart, Venus and Jupiter. Both planets are in my YOD configurations, and I have three YODs in total. YOD means Finger of God or Finger of Fate. YOD simply means a powerful dynamic aspect pattern that indicates a significant life purpose or mission. It is a fated life challenge for individuals to integrate that leads to personal growth and a deeper understanding of their path in life. Jupiter is my primary chart ruler. Jupiter governs the twelfth house, which is my filled house. Jupiter rules Sagittarius and co-rules Pisces alongside Neptune. Sagittarius is the sign of my first house, which makes me a Sagittarius rising. Scorpio is my twelfth house sign placement, which is the house where my sun resides. Both Scorpio and Pisces are water signs.

My actual Jupiter placement is in the fourth house in Aries, and Jupiter is the apex planet of one YOD. The fourth house governs family life or the home, and the gender energetic signature of the fourth house is feminine energy. The presence of Jupiter in this house highlights the profound significance of family within this fated life lesson represented by the YOD. This configuration emphasizes the destined nature of the lesson, pointing to the pivotal role of family dynamics in shaping my life's journey. Jupiter in Aries and as an apex planet signifies an abundant dynamic and assertive expansion within life. This placement indicates a drive for exploration and the pursuit of personal goals with an inclination toward fearless expression. It also indicates a strong sense of independence and leadership, with a real drive and motivation for initiating new endeavors and embracing challenges with vigor and determination. Aries rules the head, so I do tend to get headaches because of the Jupiter placement and lesson in life. I have also had five head and neck injuries that add to this life lesson.

Venus is my secondary influential chart ruler, because Venus is in its sole disposition in Libra. This is such a powerful and harmonious placement because Venus holds a dominant influence over all of the other planets in my chart, so it helps in shaping the qualities of balance, beauty, and diplomacy. Venus forms eleven aspects in my chart. Venus is also a part of one of my YOD configurations. Venus's energy is intensely integrated into my life path, so my relationships, my aesthetic sensibilities, and my pursuit of harmony are all central themes for me. This YOD points to a significant life mission involving Venusian qualities. I am compelled to resolve tensions between any challenging issues, which leads to personal growth and transformation. My life's journey is marked by the quest for balance, deep connections, and the creation of peace and beauty in my environment, reflecting the powerful influence of Venus in Libra.

The moon as the apex planet symbolizes what people call the mother wound. Having two YOD placements with the moon as the apex planet in both configurations in my chart signifies a deeply emotional and transformative life journey. The moon represents the inner world, emotions, instincts, and subconscious patterns. As the focal point of these configurations, my emotional life and intuition are under constant pressure to adapt and grow. This dual influence suggests recurring themes of emotional crisis and breakthroughs, pushing me to dive into my subconscious and understand my deepest feelings while achieving emotional maturity, literally helping me achieve emotional intelligence. These supportive sextile placements provide resources and opportunities while quincunxes create tension, requiring me to find balance and resolution in my emotional responses. This configuration indicates a powerful drive to integrate and harmonize my inner emotional world, leading to profound growth and a heightened sense of empathy and intuition. My life path is marked by significant emotional turning points, guiding me toward a deeper understanding of myself and others. In my feminine Yin life, characterized by resonance with winter solstice energies, a profound association with the maternal energies—the dark—was established due to experiencing abandonment in my early adolescence. The twelfth house, my filled house, is a house of transformation, and I carry transformer energy. I am an alchemist, and have transformed all the heavily weighted lessons I have encountered into nourishing fuel for growth in my life.

Engaging with the Akashic records is undoubtedly some of the most profound and weighted work one can undertake. It is understandable that not everyone feels compelled to dive deeply into this realm, and that is perfectly all right. Not everyone is currently living their heavy life. One way we can gain insights into our inner workings and find answers to our own questions is through the exploration of our natal birth charts. By understanding ourselves through this astrological lens, we unlock a wealth of information that can trigger profound insights from within. This self-awareness enables us to tap into our own inner wisdom and resources, allowing us to navigate our unique paths and find the answers we seek. Embracing the self-discovery journey empowers us to become our own guides, allowing us to find the clarity we need.

I won't go into all the details about how to specifically approach the Akashic records, but everything in this book will guide you to a state of openness that allows you to receive the right messages if you do decide to explore them. If you are interested in exploring these records, it is essential to do the personal work first. This foundational work will enable you to approach the records with greater clarity and a deeper understanding of yourself, your soul's path, and how your life aligns with it.

Exploring your healing and spiritual journey and seeking answers to the following profound questions requires introspection and self-awareness.

- Do I feel a calling or pull towards examining the Akashic records and, if so, how can I prepare myself for this deep exploration of universal knowledge?

- If I am struggling to find my true life path, what steps can I take to connect with my inner guidance and intuition to illuminate my purpose and direction?

- If my natal chart indicates a lack of heavy energies or significant challenges, can I find contentment in embracing the present moment without feeling pressured to work on unnecessary issues?

- In the presence of heavy energies in my birth chart, how can I prioritize and focus on where to begin clearing and healing to facilitate personal growth and transformation?

- If I engage in exploration of the Akashic records, but feel dissatisfied with the information received, how can I enhance my spiritual development to gain the awareness needed to access the answers I seek?

- How can I cultivate trust in myself to discern and validate the accuracy of the information and insights I receive from spiritual sources or practices like the Akashic records?

- If my life feels burdened by heavy karmic challenges, making it hard to experience happiness or share in others' joy, how can I work toward releasing and healing these heavy energies to foster a sense of happiness and optimism?

- If I am overflowing with joy, passion, and connectivity, making it challenging to be around those with heavy energies, how can I find a balance between honoring my own energy and empathically engaging with others without being drained?

- How do I navigate and harmonize the roles of being a receiver, transmitter, transformer, and all the facets we embody as individuals on this earthly journey to gain clarity on my purpose and contributions to the collective consciousness?

- How can I integrate spiritual practices, self-reflection, and alignment with universal laws to foster balance, self-awareness, and a sense of purpose that resonates with my authentic self so I can contribute favorably to the world around me?

CHAPTER 6:
Becoming Tuned—When Alchemy Takes Over

Alchemy encapsulates a profound philosophical and spiritual tradition, exploring the transformation of the self and the quest for spiritual enlightenment. Rooted in ancient practices, it dives into the transmutation of basic substances into prized elements, and the symbolism of this process is a metaphor for inner growth and self-realization. The aim is to transform the challenges in your life, converting the difficulties into compost that nurtures the seeds of love sown in your heart. Alchemy has deeply influenced both esoteric and scientific thought, offering layers of meaning that extend beyond the mere physical realm. When one becomes attuned to their environment and embraces the concept of alchemy, life takes on a whole new meaning. It is a journey of self-discovery and transformation where synchronicities play a significant role in shaping our experiences. This state of alignment allows us to attune ourselves with our true path, bringing us closer to our higher self.

First, let's understand the concept of synchronicity. Introduced by Swiss psychologist Carl Jung, *synchronicity* refers to *significant coincidences that occur in our lives*. These synchronicities are not just random events, but actually hold a deeper significance. When we become attuned to our environment, we start noticing these meaningful connections and understand that they are not just by chance but a reflection of the interconnectedness of everything around us. As we begin to align with our true paths, we open ourselves up to new possibilities and opportunities. By putting our intentions out into the universe, we attract the right conditions, people, and experiences that resonate with our desires and passions. This arrangement aligns us with the alchemical process, where our intentions become manifest. However, it is important to note that this journey is not always smooth sailing. Sometimes painful things arise, forcing us to confront what we are not yet ready to let go of. These challenges serve as catalysts for personal growth and transformation. They compel us to reassess our priorities and make choices that align with our true path and highest good.

Recognizing patterns in our lives is crucial for this growth. By observing these archetype patterns, we gain insights into these areas of our lives that need to change. These repeated routines can manifest in various forms, such as reoccurring relationships, habits, or experiences. Once we become aware of these schematics, we can take conscious steps to break free from old formulas and create new ones that align with our desired trajectory. Old keys will never unlock new doors. At times, the process of alignment and alchemy can be overwhelming. It requires us to let go of things that no longer serve us and to embrace new possibilities. It challenges us to question our beliefs, expectations, and attachments. However, if we stay committed to our true path and highest self, the rewards are immense. Attunement and alchemy have the power to align us with experiences, opportunities, and people that resonate with our authentic selves, ultimately leading to a more fulfilling and purposeful life.

The state of abundance is inherent to a harmoniously aligned life. Abundance and its essence has always been a state of being rather than a mere external manifestation. It represents an energetic signature, and our remarkable human bodies and brains possess the incredible ability to attune themselves to different energy frequencies, much like a satellite or a TV, changing channels to tune in to specific broadcasts. Just like tuning into a desired channel, we have the power to tap in to the vibrational frequency of abundance by consciously aligning our self with its energetic essence. This requires a deliberate and focused effort to recognize, embody, and resonate with the abundant nature of the universe surrounding us. It is through this conscious tuning and active alignment that we can tap into the limitless reservoir of abundance available to us, allowing it to flow effortlessly into our lives.

As you may have noticed, when I mention abundance I purposefully refrain from using the words wealth or money. This is because not everyone who seeks abundance is solely focused on financial gain. Upon understanding the universal principle of as above, so below and its resonance across all levels of existence from the microcosm to the macrocosm, it becomes clear that the only element that does not conform to this principle is money. Money is merely a rudimentary construct born of our primitive minds and lives. Considering that abundance is an energetic frequency accessible to us all and that energies are bound by the universal laws of cause and effect, perpetual motion, and rhythm, it becomes apparent that these energies return in cycles and whatever is put out eventually comes back.

This cycle exemplifies the energetic partnership of giving and receiving and the law of gender, where giving embodies masculine Yang energy and receiving embodies feminine Yin energy. Abundance encompasses a much broader spectrum of experiences and energies. Once we recognize that abundance exists in every moment and tap into the infinite wellspring of abundant energy provided by the earth and the universe, we begin to understand that simply existing and being present is enough.

Enough embodies the energetic signature of abundance. When you truly have enough, your life feels fulfilled. True fulfillment and living abundantly go hand-in-hand, transcending further material desires or external acquisitions in this state of fulfillment. There is no need for anything else because we are complete within ourselves. Our desires naturally arise to share this abundant feeling with others, wishing for their fulfillment as well. The act of giving, fueled by a pure heart and devoid of attachment to financial gain or specific outcomes, becomes the signature when balancing receiving energy. These two aspects harmonize and reciprocate with one another. When we give selflessly with a genuine intention for others to experience fulfillment and abundance, we also open ourselves to receiving the blessings of abundance in return.

This, in essence, is the true nature of abundance. It goes beyond monetary value and embraces the boundless flow of energy, where giving and receiving seamlessly intertwine. By cultivating a mindset of giving, free from expectations or attachments, we align ourselves with the abundant rhythms of the universe and allow abundance to naturally unfold in our lives. When we experience abundance, a natural inclination arises within us to share its blessings with others. However, I understand that accepting this concept may pose a challenge, as money has become the central focus in most people's lives. The prominence of money arises from the systematic structure that has been imposed upon us. We currently live in a late-stage hyper-capitalist society, where the emphasis is often only on becoming entrepreneurs or selling goods and services, undervaluing our worth by pursuing a job whose only interest is profit margins. Yet, a predicament arises when spirituality, for example, becomes unaffordable, as it creates a division where only the wealthy can access such wisdom. In this scenario, money assumes the role of a deity.

However, a true state of abundance spiritually allows us to share without expecting anything in return, with the sincere intention of benefiting humanity as a whole. Money should be regarded merely as a tool, not a lifestyle. Money represents a lower energetic frequency. Connecting the vibrations of giving and receiving to money without pretense can elevate its vibration. Donations, charitable deeds, and philanthropy all serve to transform the energetic signature of money. It is essential to recognize that individuals who possess great wealth without a moral compass do not necessarily contribute to the evolution of humanity; in fact, they may hinder it.

At present, the paradigm of money is not effectively serving the betterment of humanity. Many individuals have lost faith in the value of money and no longer strive solely to acquire it, which is a significant shift from the attitude of the past century. The current money-driven system, which forces humans into a form of financial slavery, does not hold the true essence of the Divine. Those who carry a pure message and seek to serve humanity from their hearts understand that sharing their wisdom is what the human species needs at this critical time. It is not about perpetuating the existing patriarchal hyper-capitalistic system that reinforces social class divisions, but rather about promoting unity and deeper connections among all individuals.

In this era of profound revolution, the Internet grants us unparalleled access to an abundant wealth of information. However, it is crucial that we develop a heightened awareness regarding the responsible and purposeful use of this knowledge. The true power lies in taking this information, internalizing it, and transforming it into wisdom. When we embody this wisdom and share it with our community, we contribute to the greater good of our species as a whole. It is essential to discern our intentions when sharing knowledge with others. If our primary motive is solely for financial gain, we inadvertently perpetuate the same broken system that currently exists. However, if we approach sharing knowledge with diligence and integrity, we can uncover individuals who, like us, are devoted to serving humanity, rather than solely serving themselves. By conducting thorough research and discernment, we can identify those who genuinely work toward the betterment of humanity. These are the individuals who diligently strive to empower others, foster unity, and create positive change. By aligning ourselves with these conscientious individuals, we can collectively work toward building a more inclusive, compassionate, and harmonious world.

The question arises to why each person's life appears to be so different if the laws of abundance in our universe hold true. To understand this, we must consider the energetic signatures imprinted upon us at birth by the planets, as well as the unique purpose of our soul in this specific body at this particular time on this planet. By consulting the Book of Life, also known as the Akashic records, we can gain insight into the interconnectedness of all energy that is required for our existence in our present form. The concept of reincarnation should inherently resonate with us, if we deeply comprehend our connection to divine energies and the eternal nature of our being. Many religions have pitched the idea of reincarnation for many millennia, so it is not a new concept. What we must grasp is that everything serves a purpose and is part of a meticulous balance. This applies not only to our planet but also on a grander scale within the mechanics of all existence.

There is a discernible pattern to our re-occurring lives, one that is governed by our karmic journey and the lessons we have learned. The experiences and events of one lifetime influence what unfolds in the next, harmonizing and equalizing the energies involved. It is important to recognize that solely cultivating a fantastic life with the expectation of favorable karma reveals a limited understanding of the whole picture. If we were born into wealth and beauty and our life was easy, it is indeed wonderful. To balance such a life, however, we must also experience hardships. This means that we might have either gone through a life that was extremely difficult and then received this blessed life because of those hardships, or we may encounter challenges in the next life. This balance is essential for promoting harmony within the grand cycle of our lives. By comprehending that our lives cycle through various stages, like the seasons on our planet, we can appreciate that some phases may be more active (Solar Yang) while others may be more receptive (Lunar Yin) within the energies of our solar system. Each of these cycles has a purpose and meaning that contributes to the overall tapestry of existence. In essence, the diversity and variations among individual lives exemplify the intricate interplay of energy required for existence. By embracing this profound interconnectedness, we get a deeper understanding of the purpose and significance inherent in every life experience.

My past life connection to Egypt emerged during a visit to the country in 2017, which I enthusiastically shared with the group I was in at the time. The trip itself was for my eleventh wedding anniversary, and it was filled with enchantment and magical occurrences—a testament to the alignment I had already cultivated in my life. Synchronicities abounded, prompting me to pay close attention to the signs and messages unfolding around me. As I journeyed through Egypt, I felt a profound connection to the land, as if the Earth herself was speaking to me through the sand and the ancient landscapes. It was during this time that I was drawn to a remarkable discovery at the Sphinx, an ancient fossil, bearing the same intricate patterns as the Flower of Life, a symbol I had permanently tattooed on my body.

The synchronicity of this finding echoed the interconnectedness of my journey and my spiritual path. Additionally, I had the privilege of having a private meditation with a pristine statue of Sekhmat. In those meditative moments, I lifted my eyelids to a moment when she seemed to smile and wink at me. The rest of my journey evoked ancient stone eyes everywhere in the rocks I found, among other artifacts that just seemed to be everywhere that I looked. These experiences felt like precious gifts, bestowed upon me by Gaia, Mother Earth herself. During my time in Egypt, I also had the opportunity to share my blood with the Nile, a deeply sacred act. Following a heartfelt prayer and blessing meditation, I turned to walk back to the van, and rain suddenly showered down from the sky, as if Egypt herself wept in my presence.

My fellow travelers became like a surrogate family, treating me like a cherished sister. My entourage hailed to me, "Egypt is crying for you, Sophora," knowing I was on my way to the airport. It was an unbelievable, yet unforgettable, moment.

Not once did the thought of exploiting the people or the culture for monetary gain cross my mind. Never did I contemplate how to profit from Egypt's rich heritage or view it as a cheap destination ripe for economic exploitation. Such notions reflect the energy of our current broken patriarchal, hyper-capitalist system, driven by individuals who seek to exploit anything, even the cultural wealth of others, solely for financial gain. Instead, my experiences in Egypt reaffirmed my commitment to integrity, respect, and reverence for the world's diverse cultures. I wholeheartedly reject the concept of exploiting any aspect of another's heritage for my own monetary benefit. This mindset aligns with a higher consciousness that fosters appreciation, preservation, and cooperation, recognizing that true richness lies in the harmonious co-existence and celebration of all of our global cultural tapestries.

These are the type of experiences that await those who engage in the transformative work and establish a deep connection with their surroundings and existence. As you align yourself with a greater flow of the universe, the universe unfolds before you, revealing new discoveries and possibilities. It is not only us who evolve; the Earth evolves alongside of us, for we are connected and a part of each other. The Earth is a master teacher and offers timeless lessons that are readily available and accessible, free of charge, at any given moment, provided that we are willing to put in the effort and do the internal work required to receive them.

When you achieve alignment, what I refer to as becoming the machine, you establish a strong connection with your higher self. This is when the words that come forth from your mouth energetically match the thought vibrations that come forth from your brain, and those will match the actions you give off into the world, which is completely authentic life engagement. Engaging in a dialogue with this aspect of yourself is essential for personal evolution. Recognizing that there exists a better version of you is important, but truly being in touch with that part of yourself takes it to another level. By actively engaging in this connection, you tap into the wisdom, guidance, and metamorphic power that your higher self offers, paving the way for profound growth and self-realization. Your life will develop or diminish according to your bravery.

Below are some questions to contemplate during your journey, ideally while in a meditative state, to attain deeper insights.

- Am I actively engaged in transforming my thoughts, emotions, and behaviors to elevate my inner self?

- Do I regularly self reflect and seek a deeper understanding of my experiences and interactions?

- Are my actions and intentions aligned with my values and higher purpose?

- Do I approach challenges and setbacks as opportunities for personal growth and evolution?

- How am I nurturing a sense of inner harmony and balance amidst life's complexities?

- Am I mindful of the energetic impact of my interactions with others and the environment?

- Do I prioritize cultivating compassion, empathy, and understanding in my relationships and daily life?

- Am I open to exploring spiritual and philosophical teachings that resonate with my inner journey?

- How do I perceive the interconnectedness of all things and the significance of this unity in my life?

- In what ways do I honor the ongoing transformation and evolution of my spiritual and emotional being?

CHAPTER 7:
Meeting the Higher Self—
A Relationship Unlike
Any Other

Meeting your higher self is a profound experience that can occur anytime throughout your life. It is a relationship unlike any other, transcending the boundaries of the physical realm and connecting us with our divine energetic essence. This encounter with the higher self opens up a pathway to deep self-reflection, spiritual growth, and a greater understanding of our purpose in the world.

When we engage in the process of alignment, we raise our level of consciousness and become more receptive to the whispers of our higher self. This inner voice, often referred to as intuition, provides guidance and insights that align with our authentic desires and highest potential. As we embark on this journey, we become increasingly aware of the wisdom and presence of our higher self. Meeting the higher self is not a single event, but rather an ongoing relationship that requires years of cultivation and nurturing. It is a sacred connection that transcends time and space, bringing us closer to the eternal aspects of our being. Through meditation, reflection, and self-inquiry, we can establish a deeper connection with that part of ourselves. One of the primary benefits of meeting the higher self is accessing profound wisdom and insight. The higher self holds a broader perspective and a deep understanding of our soul's journey. It serves as our inner guide, offering clarity and direction when we face challenges or are uncertain about the choices we need to make.

By attuning ourselves to the frequency of our higher self, we tap into this internal wellspring of wisdom and gain access to answers that are aligned with our truest selves, and it is always free. Your internal wellspring of energy never asks for money. Meeting the higher self also allows us to cultivate a sense of unconditional love and acceptance for ourselves. Our higher self knows the limitations of our human experience and has a deep compassion for our journey. It reminds us of our inherent worth and radiates a healing energy that supports our growth and transformation. This love emanates from within us, empowering us to embrace our strengths and shortcomings with kindness and forgiveness.

Furthermore, connecting with the higher self can lead to a heightened sense of purpose and alignment in life. As we deepen our relationship with this divine aspect of ourselves, we gain clarity about our passions, values, and unique gifts. The higher self acts as a compass, guiding us toward our true calling and helping us align our actions with our soul's purpose. It ignites a fire within us, inspiring us to live authentically and make choices that serve our highest good. The relationship with the higher self also fosters a sense of inner peace and serenity. When we attune to the wisdom of our higher self, we are less influenced by external circumstances and opinions. We develop a trust in the unfolding of life and embrace the concept of Divine Timing. This trust allows us to relinquish control, thereby releasing attachments and surrendering to the flow of life. We find comfort in the presence of our higher self, knowing that we are supported on every step of our journey.

Our highest self represents our light and reflects our soul's consciousness. The light is how the soul is able to move from one body to the next. Many people have had profound experiences with their light, whether through astral traveling, spiritual endeavors, or near-death experiences. These encounters offer glimpses into the essence of our being and the expansive nature of our consciousness. When we speak of our highest good or our highest self, we refer to the state in which we are aligned with our true essence, living in alignment with our authentic selves. It is the state where we embody qualities such as love, compassion, wisdom, and inner peace. Our highest good represents the highest expression of our potential and the connection to the nature of our divine consciousness.

Experiences of encountering one's light during astral traveling or near-death experiences are often described as transformative and life altering. In these states, individuals may feel a profound sense of expansion and oneness with the universe. They often describe a reunion with their true self as experiencing something that is beyond words. These encounters serve as reminders that we are more than just our physical bodies, we are beings connected to pure consciousness coming through this bodily form on this planet, right now in this moment. During astral traveling, individuals may have out-of-body experiences where their consciousness travels outside the constraints of their physical form. In these experiences, they may witness their own light or encounter higher realms of existence. It is a powerful reminder that our true essence extends beyond the limitations of the physical realm or physical body. Likewise, near-death experiences can provide profound insights into our true nature. Individuals who have come close to death may report encountering a bright light or a feeling of being enveloped in love and peace. They often describe a sense of expanded awareness and a connection to a higher power or universal consciousness.

These experiences offer a glimpse into the vastness of our being in the inherent divinity that resides within us. Encounters with our light during these experiences serve as powerful reminders of our true state and the immense potential that lies within us. They remind us that we are not separate from the divine, but rather a manifestation connected to it. These experiences offer a sense of purpose and meaning, as individuals realize the interconnectedness of all existence and the importance of living in alignment with their highest good. By embracing these experiences and recognizing the truth they reveal, we can integrate this understanding into our daily lives. We can strive to align our actions, thoughts, and intentions with our highest good, allowing our light to shine brightly into the world. This involves cultivating qualities like devotion, kindness, discernment, and making choices that are in harmony with our true selves.

Some individuals possess the remarkable ability to experience the light of their loved ones when they pass. This extraordinary phenomenon allows them to perceive the soul's essence after it departs the body, but their soul is radiant light energy. These individuals have a profound connection to the spirit realm and are able to tap in to higher frequencies where the soul of the deceased comes through as light before transitioning into another body. Experiencing the light of those who have died can bring comfort and peace to the individuals who are grieving.

An experience like this is usually only available to those who are open to this type of energy. It offers a tangible reminder that our existence extends beyond the physical realm and that the love and energy of our departed loved ones continue on. These unique individuals serve as bridges between the physical and spiritual world, offering hope and reassurance that even in death, the soul continues to endure.

I experienced one of the most difficult weeks of my life with my blood relatives the day I received the tragic news of my father's passing. I endured two difficult familial incidents during that week. This is typical of the ebb and flow of energy for my life, always receiving the most beautiful moments simultaneously with the worst. I didn't just lose my father that day; I lost a sibling as well. The profound pain of losing the only two family members I had any connection with in my bloodline weighed heavily upon me. My mother later revealed to me that my father had inquired about my whereabouts just before his passing, likely prompting his visit to me before his return back to the cycle of life's greater flow within this Great Engine.

One of my sisters called to tell me the moment he passed. As tears streamed down my face, holding my son in my arms, I called out to my father. With every repetition of, "We love you, Papa. We love you, Papa," it seemed as though my love surpassed the boundaries separating the realms of existence. In that moment, a comforting presence enveloped me and I could sense my father's light surrounding me. I could not see any physical light with my eyes open—only when I shut my eyes could I see his light—but I could feel him and sense him with my eyes open. It was as if he heard my call, responding with a love that knew no bounds. This experience eclipsed my natural world. I was able to feel his joy and his energy. I watched his energy move in and out of everything, apologizing while he was exuding the happiest energies I had ever experienced with him. He repeatedly told me he was sorry, but he was in a state of joy, almost laughing while saying he was sorry, in a dumbfounded way.

I could hear his laughter, and it brought closure and healing to our relationship. Throughout the day, my father's light lingered with me, guiding me through the process of grief and allowing us to address unresolved matters. We connected through the language of the heart, transcending words and finding understanding on a deeper level. As we connected, I was able to express my love, forgiveness, and gratitude. In that sacred space of connection, all of the lingering tensions, regret, and burdens that we had in our relationship were lifted. The weight of past misunderstandings melted away, replaced by a deep sense of tranquility. The healing power of love and forgiveness washed over me, resolving any lingering pain or resentment.

In those precious hours, I felt a deep sense of gratitude for the opportunity to have this experience and find closure. The sincere communion between my father's light and me allowed for a transformative experience of understanding and connection. We resolved everything that day, leaving no stone unturned. The weight of unfinished business was replaced by a renewed sense of peace and understanding. Throughout the day he remained by my side until I rested and closed my eyes, watching his light fade away slowly and steadily.

This extraordinary encounter provided immense clarity of purpose on my path. I went from knowing I was on a healing journey to knowing it was actually always my spiritual journey; I just hadn't understood that yet. It reinforced my views in the power of love, forgiveness, and the eternal bond of our souls' journeys. It taught me that, even in death, relationships can be healed, and it is never too late to express love and seek resolutions.

This is exactly the way to heal family karma bonds. While the pain of losing my father remains, the gift that day lingers as a testament to the healing power of love, forgiveness, and the eternal connection between us. The impact of the encounter continues to shape my journey, reminding me the immeasurable depths of the human spirit and the evolutionary potential of embracing love and compassion in all aspects of life. This life-altering experience provided guidance and clarity on my path of healing and connection. Nevertheless, it had not occurred to me that I, too, would transition into a state of light when my physical body ceased to be. It was not until the night of my extraterrestrial contact encounter that the dots of this profound realization were connected into my own life's puzzle. In a heightened state of consciousness, during a meditation, I finally made the profound connection, and the depth of that awareness washed over me. I, like all others, am a conscious light soul, connected to and a part of all that is; that will transition into a new form during rebirth.

Consider pondering the reflective questions below about your life, if you are indeed on the path to finding your light.

- Can you pinpoint a specific moment where you strongly felt that your higher self took charge?

- Have you tested your trust in yourself by asking insightful questions that only your higher self would possess the answers to?

- Have you cultivated or noticed any enhanced abilities of heightened perception or intuition?

- Do my actions and choices align with the wisdom of my higher self?

- Am I responding to situations differently? If not, have you noticed that the situations have stayed the same?

- If your situations are new, how are you responding and reacting to your new situations?

The life of a self-actualized human is characterized by a deep sense of fulfillment, purpose, and authenticity. Here are some key traits that describe the life of a self-actualized individual.

- Authenticity: A self-actualized individual is authentic and true to themselves. They have a deep understanding of their values, beliefs, and strengths, and they live in alignment with their true essence.

- Autonomy: They are self-reliant. They make choices and decisions based on their own inner guidance and have a strong sense of personal agency.

- Emotional intelligence: Self-actualized individuals possess a high level of emotional intelligence. They are aware of their own emotions and can effectively manage them. They also demonstrate empathy and understanding toward the emotions of others.

- Continued growth and learning: Self-actualized individuals have a lifelong commitment to personal growth and development. They actively seek new experiences, learning opportunities, and challenges to expand their knowledge and evolve as individuals.

- Purpose and meaning: They have a clear sense of purpose and meaning in their lives. They are guided by their core values and pursue endeavors that align with their passions and inner calling.

- Authentic relationships: Self-actualized individuals cultivate authentic and meaningful relationships. They value connection, empathy, and mutual respect in their interactions with others.

- Self-acceptance: They have a deep acceptance of themselves, including their strengths and weaknesses. They embrace their imperfections and view them as opportunities for growth rather than sources of shame or self-judgment.

- Connection with the present moment: Self-actualized individuals have a heightened sense of presence. They are fully engaged in the present moment, appreciating the beauty and richness of their experiences, without being lost in the past or consumed by worries about the future.

- Altruism and compassion: They demonstrate a genuine concern for the well-being of others and engage in acts of kindness and compassion. They understand the interconnectedness of all beings and actively contribute to the betterment of their communities and to the world at large.

Self-actualization is an ongoing journey rather than a destination. It is a continuous process of growth and self-discovery, and individuals may exhibit these behaviors to varying degrees, depending on their personal development.

When a person becomes self-actualized and lives authentically, it naturally reflects in their life. They radiate a uniqueness and truth that is unmistakably their own. Their actions, choices, and interactions with others are a true reflection of their authentic self. By embracing their individuality, they create a life that is genuine and aligned with their values, dreams, and passions. Their truth shines through in all aspects of their life, creating an undeniable impact on their relationships, pursuits, and overall fulfillment, especially within the self.

There will be occasions when individuals desire to test their higher selves to build a greater confidence in this realm. Some may have inquiries for their higher selves once they have complete trust in themselves. In either scenario, the higher self possesses superior knowledge compared to our human minds. They have witnessed all of our lifetimes and were present at every one of our births.

Warning: Graphic Content Section

I embarked on my first remote viewing experience in a group setting, which brought about a great sense of accomplishment when I was the only one who performed correctly. This remarkable event is further detailed in Chapter 9 of my journey. It instilled within me a newfound confidence, empowering me to trust my higher self with even the most intimate inquiries. With trust firmly established under my metaphorical belt, I felt a compelling need to dive deeper into understanding my own essence.

This led me to courageously seek clarity from my higher self about serious aspects of my personal journey, including the sacred topic of my virginity. Through this exploration, I embarked on a path of self-discovery and complex understanding with my connection to myself. I have lived a life of heavy karma, so bear with me.

As a woman, I hold within me the most powerful tool available to humankind: The womb. It is responsible for birthing every individual into existence, including your higher self. In a traumatic memory, my sacred vessel—my womb—became a hot topic of unsettling conversation. At eleven years old, I found myself confronted by the elders of my parents' cult. I had been rebelling against them and my parents. Having to witness the elders and leaders in the cult degrade and abuse young girls as well as cover up such behavior within their organization served as the primary reasons why I chose not to remain there or emulate anyone I had known there, leading me to rebel.

Why I was rebelling and what I did to rebel—I did plenty of stupid things—is multi-faceted, which will require another book all on its own. Mostly, I longed for freedom and my own identity; I really did not want to be a part of their organization. They questioned me intently about what I had been doing, because I was considered a runaway. They threatened to take a look for themselves to check if I was a virgin. I was already aware that I had nothing to find. People had already tried to find it . . . including me.

My first memory is from when I was around six years old. I was spending the night with a girl who was about a year older than me, but from the same cult; we were at her grandparents' house. She asked me to do to her what she did to me, but I didn't want to. I was horrified, in a state of shock, wiggling my way free from her grip. Luckily, her grandmother came in and saved me when it was supposed to be my turn. Looking back, it is obvious that she did to me what someone else did to her. Regardless, the trauma from it was always in my head. There was never any blood. The second memory is from when I was eleven years old. A strange boy appeared in my bedroom window, claiming that a relative's friend had sent him to fetch me. I had never seen him before. He pulled me out of my window and forced me onto the ground, creating an extremely unsettling situation. The violation and assault lasted briefly—he left abruptly and upset when he put his hand between my legs, using his fingers to look for blood, but found none. He left me there on the ground and didn't say another word before leaving me there in a state of despair and disbelief.

I had looked back on both of those experiences, wondering, because both incidents were without blood. This is why I wanted to ask my higher self. When I settled down to meditate on this matter, I approached it with an open mind, uncertain of what to anticipate. Yet, I held trust in the process; I knew that if anyone had the answer to this question, she did. As I connected with my inner light during my meditation, I immediately posed my question to her in thought, not even getting to finish the question. Without a moment's hesitation, she responded with a clear answer. Instantaneously, a surge of energy transported me into a particular memory that had been inaccessible to me until that point because of my young age, but it was retained by her.

The only words she screamed with urgency to me were "Shark bite!!!" before immersing me in that stored memory.

Those who know me are well aware of my torment involving sharks. Night after night when I was a child, I was plagued by the horrifying scenario of being devoured by those aquatic predators. I emphasize the frequency by stating that this occurred every single night throughout my entire existence as a child. As I matured into adulthood, however, the nightmares involving sharks became less frequent, occurring only sporadically, and then stopped after I had my son when I was thirty-two. Nevertheless, the sharks never failed to manifest. As a child, I met my demise at the jaws of a shark night after night, with the terrifying creatures even transforming into robotic forms to pursue me on land.

As soon as I heard "Shark bite!!!" I immediately went into a state of knowing, claircognizance. I was just around two years old at the time, yet the memory of that moment eluded me until I asked my higher self. It provided me with more than I could have anticipated, and I am forever grateful that I finally understand it all now.

My first abuser had a door in his house that was adorned with various types of locks from top to bottom; I would say a few dozen at least. His house was old, worn down, and had cracks all over it—doors, walls, everything. He told me that he kept sharks locked up down there, and that they would get me if I got too close. It was a warning meant to keep me away from him, but it did not work. I was just a curious toddler wanting attention, so I went to sit in his lap. In that typical childish act, he stole my sacred innocence.

The next time he saw me, he laughed at me for keeping my distance and tauntingly reminded me, "See, I told you those sharks bite."

After receiving a plethora of information during my personal affirmations, I made a conscious decision to shift my focus toward gaining clarity on specific matters. I dove deeply into my Akashic records because I yearned to understand more about my father's side of the family. I had always felt a closer bond with my father. He was willing to show vulnerability, apologize, and express remorse after incidents, even though the organization he was part of told him to discipline his children through physical means. I was repeatedly reminded that their Bible said to beat your children with a rod if they do not obey. I always felt strange that they could justify physically harming their children when it's illegal to do that to adults. How can anyone justify physically hurting a small child when we are told to obey the government, which explicitly states that we should not harm one another? Some people twist religious teachings to rationalize beating their children when they don't comply, claiming that God approves of such actions. It raises a profound question: Why would God advocate for harming children, but not for harming adults? This contradiction made me realize that they are misinterpreting the principles of the God they claim to serve, leading to inconsistencies in their understanding of their own Bible.

Nevertheless, my father demonstrated regret for his actions. On the other hand, my mother was the one making decisions and issuing orders, including those related to discipline. Our relationship was always better because my father would sincerely apologize to me, whereas my mother never admitted her mistakes or showed vulnerability by offering apologies at all; all she ever expressed were excuses about why she made her decisions and standing firm in them. It's unusual to think that my father was the one who physically disciplined me, yet he maintained a closer relationship with me due to his genuine remorse. My mother never physically harmed me, but she denied any emotional connection to the abuse I experienced, consistently stating that she refused to feel bad about it.

My father had a complex upbringing. I was told that his father was born during the whitewashing of America on an Oklahoma reservation and belonged to the Choctaw tribe. The only time I witnessed my father explore his Native American heritage was when his health started to decline. He wanted free healthcare, and believed that Native Americans were entitled to such benefits. However, he discovered that he would need to live on the reservation to receive those services. He was the youngest of eight children. He grew up around the reservation boundaries. He was born four years before his father's death. Without a true connection to his father, he grew up listening to the stories shared about him by his brothers. Stories from my father's childhood revolved around his father being a moonshiner during Prohibition. Due to his father's mixed heritage of being half native Choctaw blood and half white man blood, he was given a name with an identifier of his mixed blood. I wasn't aware that the name carried such a history of shame until I embarked on my spiritual journey, tapping into my higher self and seeking answers within the Akashic records. It became apparent that generations of family karma had been passed down, and someone like me was fated to emerge, recognize it, and work toward releasing and healing it.

The similarities between my life and my grandfather's life are uncanny. I don't believe in coincidences, I believe that coincidences are synchronicities that we need to be paying attention to. Everything happens for a reason, and everything happens in its Divine Time.

These experiences with my higher self strengthened my inner confidence and transformed my intuitive abilities into my own personal super powers. Once I started utilizing my super powers, I initially used them for selfish purposes. I had an insatiable thirst for knowledge, and would ask questions that I did not necessarily need answers to. I soon realized that not all memories or information proved beneficial. Each individual has the capacity to handle what their present moment holds in their minds. Each moment in time serves as a gateway to further experiences, revealing interconnectedness through the multi-verse. However, understanding this intricate web of connections requires effort and diligence.

It is necessary to embark on your personal journey ascending the ladder of success one rung at a time. I began to question my higher self about why I hadn't been able to possess this knowledge earlier. In response, she reminded me that I had been trapped in a victim mindset and unable to comprehend and utilize the information for my betterment as I could now. My higher self emphasizes the concept of Divine Timing to me a lot. This reminder holds particular significance for me due to my Stellium and filled twelfth house, located in Scorpio. The focal point lies in the twelfth house, which is governed by Jupiter, Neptune, and Pisces.

I am what they call Neptunian. With five energies expressing in the twelfth house, the most crucial aspects of my life are meant to unfold in my later years. This astrological forecast is already manifesting, as I have learned my most profound lessons at the age of forty-four. Now, at forty-eight, I have processed my experiences, I am reflecting, and now I am writing about them. I would say that these are my later years, and my focus has never been so crystal clear. My experiences wouldn't have happened unless I had lived the allotted time for them all to unfold in their own Divine Time.

If you are contemplating Divine Timing in your own life and reflecting upon past experiences, these questions might help you on your journey.

- What signs indicate that I am aligned with Divine Timing in my endeavors?
- How does trust in Divine Timing influence my perception of life's unfolding events?
- In what ways can I cultivate patience and acceptance of Divine Timing on my journey?
- What practices support my attunement to the rhythms of Divine Timing?
- What role do I believe Divine Timing has played in shaping my major life events?
- Have I ever felt conflicted between my own plans and what I perceive as Divine Timing?
- In moments of uncertainty or impatience, how do I trust in Divine timing?
- Do I believe that setbacks or delays could be a part of Divine Timing's plan for my life?
- How does reflecting on Diving Timing influence my approach to decision-making and goal setting?
- Can I recall a time when Divine Timing brought unexpected blessings or opportunities into my life?

CHAPTER 8:
Connect for Contact— My Extraterrestrial Contact Visitation

As I sit down to write this chapter, the clock shows 1:44 p.m., a number that has held deep significance in my life for many years. It has become a sacred symbol, appearing repeatedly throughout my days and marking moments of great meaning. I have skipped ahead a bit in the writing process to tackle this chapter, as it is one that flows easily for me. It brings relief, lessening the burden of the work of writing this book that lay ahead.

This particular experience holds unparalleled importance, imprinting itself into my memory from the moment I woke up that morning. Writing a book is no small task. It is an overwhelming experience that encompasses the culmination of my life's story, intertwined with extraordinary encounters that taught me more than any other experience ever could. Attempting to convey this information in a linear fashion proves challenging, as the contents of this book defy traditional writing conventions. It is more than simply recounting events; it is an energetic display of the complex events that shaped my life, leading to the incredible gift of the contact experience.

I have had two other unusual experiences with origins in the E.T. or UFO genre already in my life, but nothing that compared to my experience on the night of October 23, 2020. My memory of the evening I had just experienced, from the time I first opened my eyes the next morning, remains etched deep within me. What I'm about to share defies conventional storytelling, as it dives into the realms of the extraordinary and inexplicable. It takes us beyond the realm of the known and into uncharted territory.

As I recount this experience, I am reminded of the immense responsibility that comes with writing a book of this nature. It is not just a retelling of events; it is an invitation to explore the depths of your own consciousness, to investigate the mysteries that lie beyond our perception. It is an opportunity to challenge our preconceptions, to question the limitations we have placed upon ourselves, and to embrace the extraordinary possibilities that appear before us. Throughout the journey of writing this book, I have come to understand that there is no linear path when it comes to exploring the depths of our own existence. The chapters within this book are interconnected, intertwining our personal narratives with the cosmic tapestry that unites us all. Each chapter offers a fragment of the whole, a facet of the truth that remains elusive in its entirety. It is an exploration of consciousness, of our connection to the Divine Energy that permeates all of our existence, and of the mystical experiences that defy logic and reason that our humans brain can understand in its current stage. This particular chapter, however, allows us to momentarily step off the path of exploration and immerse ourselves in the vivid recollection of a singular experience. By narrating this chapter in a somewhat linear fashion, I can paint a clearer picture of the events that transpired and the impact they had on my life.

Allow me to begin by recounting the week leading up to the contact experience. I had embarked on a solo retreat, seeking solitude and reflection. For this purpose, I took refuge in my travel trailer, finding peace in its familiarity and the convenience of its hook ups that allowed me to have a place for uninterrupted, meditative states. Throughout my life, I have felt the ebb and flow of energy, noting how the most extraordinary experiences were often balanced by challenging times and vice versa. This understanding of the intricate balance of energy within my life sent me into self-healing mode, propelling me into harnessing the culmination of various healing modalities I had acquired over the years. During this period of time, I was already immersed in a program aimed at deepening my connection with the celestial regents, the celestial bodies that hold sway in our lives. It was a natural progression after my astrology program that offered profound insight into myself and into my loved ones.

The knowledge gained through astrology nurtured not only a deeper understanding of myself but also strengthened the bonds I shared with others. This course was another step on my educational journey, which had consumed most of my time over the past decade. I was already certified in integrative medicine, holistic health, Reiki, nutrition, herbology, and astrology; now I was determined to deepen my relationship with the planets, the signs of the zodiac, the houses of the zodiac wheel, and the angelic energies that preside over these celestial temples. As I neared the end of the program, I found myself in the month of Uranus, one of the planets that happens to reside in my twelfth house in Scorpio. I had a profound experience that left an incredible mark on my conscious awareness.

During the guided meditation session, like all the rest, the visualization led to the merging of my light, which represented my highest self. In my third eye, I witnessed the silhouette of my face emerging from the veil of light as I merged with my true self. The program had been an eighteen-month immersion, and I anticipated that profound shifts would occur within me as a result of my dedicated efforts. It was something I had come to expect, having experienced transformative moments throughout similar intensive journeys. However, seeing my face appearing within the veil of light during the meditation evoked a sense of joy, as if I had uncovered a treasured secret of my existence. During the rest of the eighteen months, and all of the guided meditations I participated in, the silhouette of my face was never embossed in the light before. It had been a familiar meditative journey, as I merged with my soothing light energy before proceeding further to meet with the planet, house, angels, and energies of them all. Merging with my light energy had been a consistent part of my meditation practice for a least the past thirteen years to that point. I believe this practice over time gave me the firm foundation I needed with my true self that eventually led me to this contact experience.

True to the intricate dance of karma that shapes my life journey, the balance of energy swiftly saw equilibrium. Balancing energetic forces quickly manifested themselves, presenting me with new life challenges that tested my resilience. While I now understand the significance of these experiences and view them as gifts, at the time the events unfolded I felt a surge of anger and found myself reacting impulsively in those moments. I failed to embody the knowledge that I possessed, acting as a victim rather than an empowered individual who had learned to navigate life's adversities. It is within the grand mechanics of the universe that the lessons we need to learn are woven and teachers are brought forth to provide the necessary guidance. The key rests in our willingness to receive the lessons and integrate them into our lives.

This, however, was the most important lesson I had yet to learn, despite my difficult past and upbringing—a true testament to the transformative nature of my journey. The events that unfolded during this time challenged me to dig deeper, to question my reactions, and to rise above the limitations I had placed upon myself. Though the lessons may have been delivered through contrasting energies, I now recognize the loving intentions behind them. Through acceptance and openness, I embraced the wisdom they imparted and committed myself to learning and growth. As I reflect upon the unique tapestry of my journey, I am reminded of the constant interplay between polarity and harmony, light and darkness, lightness and density. It is through our experiences, both easy and challenging, that we gain a deeper understanding of ourselves in the world around us. Each lesson serves as an invitation to shed old patterns and beliefs, and to embrace the limitless potential that resides within. With gratitude and an open heart, I embarked upon the path that lay before me—an ever-evolving quest for self-discovery, transformation, and connection with my true self: my inner light soul.

My meditation retreat was nestled in the comfort of my camper trailer in my backyard. I found myself grappling with intense emotions. Experiencing anger, reactivity, and a sense of powerlessness for the past four weeks had consumed me. At the time, I had thirteen years of dedicated healing work, but in that moment, everything I had learned to embody slipped away. It left me yearning to rediscover my true self, yet again. I pulled back into my camper for nearly a week, immersing myself in meditation. It was Friday, October 23, 2020, marking the end of the week since I had started my journey of meditation. Throughout the week, I had been diligently exploring my emotions and making a conscious effort to adhere to an anti-inflammatory diet, cleansing my body of toxins. Drawing from the wealth of knowledge and tools I had acquired over the past decade, I knew I possessed the means to heal myself.

Amidst the turmoil, I became increasingly aware of a part within me that remained untouched by anger. This part exuded control and unconditional love, and I began to engage in a dialogue with her. Throughout my journey, I had encountered her numerous times, but this was the first time I asked her for her assistance. I asked for my inner light to manifest and guide me through this period of suffering. From the depths of my heart, I begged for guidance and liberation from the goings-on that were causing me pain and suffering. Tears flowed as I expressed my desire to heal. I was desperate to free myself from this baggage, as through its dissolution I would propel myself toward true unconditional love and forgiveness.

The religious environment I grew up in professed to offer unconditional love, but what they actually taught was that their love was conditional—only given if you served, obeyed, and were subservient to them and their rules. This is the true definition of conditional love. I longed to understand what unconditional love really meant, and while I thought I had it in my adult life, my entire experience was about developing and grasping its true essence; not just for myself but also for those I love the most. This is what I wanted to embody.

With upmost vulnerability, I asked my higher self for assistance, willing to undertake any task or risk necessary to alleviate not only my shame and anger but that of the person I most dearly loved. I never had a supportive family to talk to, which makes navigating life alone particularly challenging. I experienced guilt about my best friends because I heavily depended on them in the past. I wanted to become a more complete and supportive friend to them, like they had been to me, rather than constantly relying on them during my tough moments.

I thought back to my father, the only parent with whom I shared any true connection. Despite his parenting style that involved physical discipline, he also displayed an unparalleled capacity for vulnerability. He consistently followed the orders of his leaders, yet he frequently expressed regret and apologized to me for his actions. His vulnerability toward me strongly influenced our relationship. At that moment, all I could focus on was wishing he was there to talk to me, but all I had were memories. Memories of his light passing intertwined with my own memory of my light emerging through the veil during my meditation. Suddenly, the pieces began to click into place. I had failed to realize that if my father transformed into pure light energy after his body passed, so did I. In that moment of meditation, I had witnessed my own face merging with the veil of light, solidifying my understanding that I, too, am light, an external extension of consciousness, able to have a life in this evolved body on this planet.

These revelations unfolding during my meditation expanded my awareness exponentially. I, at that moment, embodied full Divine Consciousness; I was aware of who I truly was while in my human form and my light form. Fueled by this realization, I called out to my higher self, acknowledging her existence and drawing upon her strength. I asked her for her help. When I requested guidance from my higher self on healing my pain and suffering, she indicated that I was struggling with and suffering from attachments, a concept linked with Buddhism. Upon learning of these attachments, I agreed that it made total sense, and I begged her to help me release these attachments. So, she did! She released me from the weight of these attachments during the meditation, and I got to experience an ethereal weightlessness, an overwhelming sense of bliss, deeply anchoring me into my relationship with her. However, this state was fleeting, as she then revealed that all human suffering emanates from attachments—attachments to people, things, ideas, and expectations. Suddenly, I was carrying the burden of the collective suffering, and it was almost unbearable. I yearned to understand how to aid others in helping them release their attachments as well, driven purely by my compassionate electromagnetic heart resonance.

Since I was in a state of understanding—that I was light consciousness—and the immense burden of the pain and suffering I had just experienced from the collective, I asked her to reach out to other beings of light, seeking their support in this task. The presence of my father's light energy in my mind gave me the encouragement and guidance to ask this of my own light consciousness. My father was the one I was reaching out for when I called forth other beings of light. I am fully aware of the existence of angels, guides, and energies that individuals believe have a significant presence and protect them in their lives. We have called upon our ancestors in prayer to help guide us as long as we have had written history. As I sat in my true form, fully embodying it, I felt the collective burden lift and a sense of peace and weightlessness enveloped me.

Even though the pain of the collective suffering went away, my meditative conversation never truly ceased; rather, it transformed into an internalized reality check, unlocking latent aspects within myself. I have no recollection of actually lying down and falling asleep; all I remember is this blissful, peaceful state and the tranquility I was experiencing. I felt like I had entered an alternate dimensional state of being, where pure love radiated from my heart. In this state, I was tuned in to my true self, having fully embodied her. I suppose I fell asleep, even though I do not recall doing this. All I remember was my peaceful state and my surroundings.

I had meticulously arranged my camper space—an altar adorned with a diffuser emanating my exotic hand-blended essential oils and my geometric crystal grid strategically positioned for open communication, among many sacred objects that I strategically placed since they hold deep significance to me. However, it was the assortment of stones I had gathered from all corners of the globe that dominated the altar, representing the anchor of my spiritual practice. Stone has always spoken to me.

In the midst of the night, unaware of what time it was, I awoke with an incredible sense of alertness. There was no grogginess or confusion; my mind was sharp, my eyes focused. I saw them instantly: a Being inside my trailer. There was no doubt in my mind—there was an extraterrestrial being standing just a few feet away from me. It was as if the Being activated my consciousness, ensuring that I would remember this experience. At that moment, the Being was not directly facing me. I was laying on my right side, and the table in the camper obstructed my view of the lower half of its body. However, the top half of the being was in clear sight, four to five feet away. It wore what appeared to be a typical green suit, and its distinct features included large black eyes. What caught my attention was a black tube-like structure extending from the back of its head, curving around and disappearing back into the suit.

The Being was gazing ahead in the direction of my refrigerator, providing me only a side profile view of the top half of their body at the beginning of the encounter. The Being slowly began to turn its head toward me, in what felt like extreme slow motion. Without hesitation, I attempted to establish communication. Countless questions flooded my mind instantaneously, though they never materialized as spoken words—rather, they were thoughts. The Being responded telepathically to my thoughts, mostly through images and occasional telepathic statements. Every time I tried to rise from my position, the Being assured me that I was safe and repeatedly reminded me that I was not afraid. My barrage of questions began with skepticism. Is this really happening? Why is this happening to me? Why here? Why now? Why aren't you communicating with the governments? Why are you here? Why me?!?

The Being swiftly responded to each inquiry. When I questioned why was this happening to me, they showed me a mental image of myself meditating in the camper and conveyed that I had asked for assistance. They revealed that my true self had asked for it. That is true, I asked her to reach out to other beings of light to help me. When I asked them why here, the Being presented me with a mental image of stored weapons inside the home in the safe, conveying that they avoid environments where fear may prevail, as it hinders human evolution, basically saying that the location and environment gave them the ability since it was safe for both of us. Regarding communication with the governments, the Being began a rapid telepathic data transfer, as if delivering a mental download, because my awareness lacked the knowledge of why they would be in my presence.

Meanwhile, my mind continued to race with questions and the Being was still slowly turning its head in my direction. Twice I requested a closer encounter, looking for a more personal connection. However, both times I was met with a calming sensation and reassurance that I was safe and had no reason to fear. I repeatedly affirmed, "I know I am not afraid!" I longed for a greater physical presence, yearning for control over my body and a more intimate encounter.

Recounting the passage of time is difficult, as the Being's slow head movement seemed to stretch out the moments during my mental data download. Amid the rapid flow of questions and downloaded information, it felt as if time stood still for me; those few seconds (more than likely) seemed to stretch on forever. Instantaneously, my most pressing life questions were answered, yet an infinite cascade of new questions arose within me. I realized that this experience was forging new pathways in my brain and my body, an understanding that still resonates with me today. I comprehended that this moment was a gift, and all I could offer in return was heartfelt gratitude. When the Being finally met my gaze, a surge of energy pulsed between us, I felt this intense power in our eye contact, and then the Being closed my eyes while leaving my awareness intact. I pleaded for the encounter not to end, being fully aware and awake but suspended in absolute darkness. All I knew was that I did not want this extraordinary experience to end.

It became clear to me that the Being's large black eyes were more equivalent to high-tech sunglasses embedded in its Earth spacesuit, utilizing advanced technology. It possessed the ability to control everything in my trailer that evening through the technology harnessed within those big black lenses.

I know many will be curious about whether my father was involved in this encounter. All I can say is that if he were involved, I would have recognized that. I've never felt that connection, although it is possible. I simply don't have the feeling that he was present, nor did they give me the awareness that he was present. I think he has already moved on to his next journey. Instead, it was those who governed the area at the time, overseeing humanity's evolution, who I was able to contact because I was in a higher dimensional state of being. They could assist me due to the circumstances. But no, I do not have the awareness that my father was a part of my encounter that evening at all.

The duration of the time that I was suspended in complete darkness during the second phase remains unknown to me. When I was conscious, it became a whirlwind of countless contemplations swirling within my mind. Describing it would be like having conscious awareness suspended in weightlessness and emptiness, but also darkness; aware of everything, just without feeling the burdens of my humanity. There was zero fear there; in fact, there was zero fear in the entire encounter. In that moment, it was just my thoughts and me, fully aware of the extraterrestrial visit I had just experienced, contemplating the revelations and visions I had received via the mental download.

Then came a period that I was in a state of pure emptiness, void of any thoughts or contemplation whatsoever. I had requested the continuation of the experience; my wish was granted. However, narrating the latter part of my encounter required reflection and a deeper understanding of what transpired. In my limited human form and with my limited cognitive faculties, comprehension eluded me at the time. It was only after meditating and contemplating the experience that the pieces of the puzzle began to fit together, revealing the true nature of what had occurred.

When I regained consciousness, the intensity of the light around me was immediately overwhelming. I was effectively blinded, struggling to make sense of my surroundings. Everything appeared distorted, hazy, and strangely overly bright. As I shifted my gaze upward, the brightness gradually diminished to a more tolerable level. However, when I directed my sight downward toward my own body, it was as if I was staring into the sun, an overwhelming brilliance that I could not fully comprehend. My eyes instinctively avoided the lower perspective, focusing instead on the less intense light above me. It was then that I began to discern the presence of Beings approaching me. Initially, I could only make out their heads as they drew near, but soon enough their faces became clearly visible. These were Beings with a humanoid appearance, but different. They lacked hair and possessed disproportionately large eyes, but were still humanoid. Their eyes were not completely black like they had been in the camper; they were just large and overdeveloped. That is how I knew they were indeed wearing a spacesuit in my camper.

Their skin, almost grey in complexion, retained a familiar resemblance to humanity. I understood that they were not a product of evolution or development under our sun. There were approximately five or six of them, silently communicating with me—their lips moving, their intentions seemed clear. My attention was absorbed by the extraordinary luminosity surrounding me. Reflecting upon this now, I understand that my inability to hear them was a consequence of existing in my state of light. Although I turned my head, or what seemed like turning my head, the intensity of the light kept compelling me to avert my gaze. Looking upward was the only way I could manage to see their faces. The light was just so intense that focusing was very strenuous. I kept trying to regain a better focus and have a communicative experience with them, shifting my perception frequently. I was trying to figure out how to navigate the experience. I could sense them and their desire for me to have a peaceful experience, but I was too focused on trying to have some type of control over my functions. They knew I felt frustrated by my inability to speak to them, hear them, or move my body. As I looked above, at the less intense light, I caught a glimpse of darkness beyond. Intrigue directed my attention toward it, as if instinctively following its pull. The movement, or what felt like movement, involved turning my head over my right shoulder, revealing a view of my physical body. There I lay, within the confines of my camper, around forty to fifty feet below.

Observing my body from this altered state, I experienced a sense of calm and contentment. I understood that I had just encountered extraterrestrial beings, and here I was, now connected to them and in contact with them again. My body lay safely beneath me, and a feeling of tranquility washed over me. I gently closed what I thought were my eyes, because the intensity of the light was almost unbearable. I found relief in this calmness that the Beings had thought to instill within me.

The intricacies of how they facilitated the second part of the experience remain elusive to me. Through deep meditation and contemplation, I have come to the realization that they brought my light consciousness, my light soul, to where ever they resided; yes, more than likely their spaceship. This would allow them to provide the assistance I had asked for during my meditation session. Their advanced Earth spacesuit technology played a role in orchestrating this encounter. This is comparable to astral traveling, although I was never in control; they guided the entire experience. They emphasized that my active role in initiating contact played a vital part in enabling this interaction. This was not a random visitation; it was a deliberate opportunity for them to demonstrate the possibilities that arise when genuine contact is established.

I understand that there are limitations to what they can do, hence the distinct difference between the first and second halves of the encounter. They ensured that I could comprehend the purpose and significance of the experience, going above and beyond what I had initially requested. They entrusted me with a wealth of information, including a vast amount of downloaded data. Processing the enormity of this encounter took me two years. The experience itself, combined with the subsequent integration of the downloaded information, offered an unparalleled opportunity for growth and understanding. I will be working on assimilating this information for the rest of this life on Earth.

The gateway to endless questioning lies within the infinite expanse of knowledge. A vast number of questions unfurls, awaiting exploration and understanding. To grasp this concept fully, one must open their own being to the infinite possibilities and expand their own conscious awareness. Empowering oneself with expanded consciousness is a pivotal step toward assimilating an abundance of information. The necessary energetic foundation already exists; we simply need to align ourselves and allow for that connection. Our conscious awareness holds the key to our evolution, a responsibility diligently overseen by extraterrestrial beings. Guiding and supporting human evolution is their primary objective. Our cognitive capability, operating at a mere fraction of its true capacity, shows that our potential remains untapped. Remarkable things have been achieved even while we are using our limited potential, underscoring the immense possibilities waiting to be unlocked.

Personal research and endeavors have led me to explore the realms of human evolution, a journey that will be discussed in subsequent chapters. Human evolution is the driving force behind our existence, as well as theirs. We were brought into existence to advance the species, a motive shared by countless other civilizations and species. For any species, progression stems from the desire to enhance genetics. The principles of genetics reveal the importance of quantity—a larger sample size increases the odds of success in any scientific genetic experiment. Consequently, billions of us exist on earth, providing an ideal environment for the refinement of advanced genetic material.

Habitable planets brimming with life are not a rarity. The quest for evolution transcends our boundaries and reaches far beyond our extraterrestrial confines. Their evolution spans the vastness of space. We go through this transformative process multiple times, beginning as conscious energy in light form before embarking on this earthly venture. Energy permeates everything, a universal constant in constant motion and transformation. It is an inherent quality deeply ingrained within all things, a fundamental universal law, understood and taught by ancient civilizations. Yin and Yang together signifies a balanced energetic existence and serves as a symbol that is universally recognized. Throughout our existence, we have embarked on a shared evolutionary journey with this planet, refining the bodies we inhabit—our Earth space suits. We are intertwined, inseparable from the intricate fabric of the Earth. Nurturing our embodied experiences offers us the opportunity to progress alongside the planet. Our success in this endeavor thus far serves as a testament to our ability to evolve, a testament we will continue to bolster. In the current era, the evolution of consciousness takes precedence, a captivating subject that will be explored further in later chapters.

The intricacies of this topic generate a plethora of questions, a cascade of inquiries that intrigue and inspire. As to whether they provide a definite answer regarding the conscious evolution of humans, the answer—they told me—lay in our hearts. The nature of this subject matter is multifaceted, interwoven with the complexities of our environment, our brains, and the multitude of factors that shaped our lives. There is no singular answer; it is an intricate and unique concept. They also disclose the significance of sound. Though sound may appear to be a vague term, its importance is undeniable. Sound served as a vital tool in our initial evolution, as it formed the foundation for language and communication amongst ourselves. Harnessing sound now necessitates an inward shift, encompassing communication with our bodies. Untapped potential lies within, awaiting discovery and realization. This focus on the untapped potential of sound serves as the focal point of my present work, exploring its myriad forms and applications.

Sound is thought to have been initiated by women, because they were the ones who stayed together with the children while men went out to hunt. During the hunt, communication among men would have been minimal, prompting women to create their own language to share resources and teach children, and to share discoveries with one another. Women have played a crucial role in the evolution of humankind, especially considering that all fetuses start as female; the shift to male occurs in the womb of a female during the third month or ninth week of pregnancy, under specific conditions. This scientific discovery began as a theory in 1951, but has since been accepted as fact, even though it was suppressed by men who didn't want it to be known. The influence of the unbalanced patriarchal era contributed to this oversight. This insight is further detailed in the book *The Great Cosmic Mother*, which highlights the historical significance of women's contributions to language, society, and the evolution of humankind.

The Beings communicated to me that it was the pure, loving, altruistic intent emanating from deep within my heart's resonance that had led me to the dimension where contact with them was possible. With intentions driven by the utmost love and the unwavering desire to heal not only my own suffering but also that of others, I was given this gift of contact in the dimension where they are able to communicate with us. Determining the purity of your intentions requires undertaking the necessary work to cultivate and expand our consciousness. This transformative process unfolds naturally, serving as an inherent outcome of the inner work that each individual commits to. As we deepen our connection with ourselves and elevate our consciousness, we elevate our energetic vibration, thus raising the vibrational state of our entire experience. Our thoughts align harmoniously with our actions and our actions seamlessly align with our words. In turn, our words reflect the very thoughts that permeate our being, ultimately shaping the reality that we manifest.

When we reach and maintain this state of alignment, we tap into the abundant flow of high-frequency vibrations that exist within and around us. Life itself, in all its dynamic expressions, dances and moves, echoing the celestial rhythms of the planets and the fundamental essence of energy. It is through the diligent practice of cultivating strategies and adapting to the ebb and flow of life that we are able to navigate through our most significant growth periods. Life holds within it both ease and challenges. It is in those moments of challenge that we are offered tremendous opportunities for growth and expansion. Though it may take time to fully appreciate this, once we immerse ourselves in the exploration of our own internal landscapes, we can better understand the intricate workings of karma. Life often introduces stressors that we may not immediately comprehend, stressors that have their origins in past actions and the interplay of the universal law of cause and effect. This emphasizes the importance of engaging in the necessary inner work, to deepen our understanding and prepare ourselves for the journey that lies ahead.

It is worth noting that each individual's karmic journey is distinct. While some may have lighter burdens to bear, others may find themselves grappling with heavier and more deeply ingrained patterns. Each person's journey through life is comprised of a delicate interplay of cyclical patterns, echoing the ceaseless revolution of the zodiac and the ever-shifting seasons of the year on the planet. All is cyclical, interdependent, and interconnected; each component intricately interwoven into the grand tapestry of existence, the Great Engine. Our exponential journey on this planet is an embodiment of our revolutionary process, where we refine and evolve these earthly vessels we inhabit. In reality, we are not separate from this planet; our very essence is intricately woven into the fabric of the earth. By fully embracing the embodiment of our experiences and consciously evolving alongside the planet in harmony, we will continually evolve the body in which we navigate this journey. Our collective success in refining and advancing the human form, however, hinges upon our conscious evolution. The chapter that ultimately deals with conscious evolution will unravel the multifaceted complexities that arise within this context.

By delving into the depths of our own consciousness, unlocking our DNA, and imbuing it with new light technology and codes, we embark on a path of transformation and enlightenment. Our true nature, our inherent enlightenment, is love. However, grasping the depths and essence of this truth is a personal journey, one that requires profound introspection. Many have yet to fully comprehend the depths of unconditional love, remaining firmly rooted in conditional forms of love. True enlightenment comes when we are able to see ourselves reflected in everyone, embracing and loving others as we love ourselves, but it all starts with self-love. There must be zero judgments, comparisons, expectations, pretense, masks, and deceit, and only acceptance, like that of a new baby finding its way in its new form. This heartfelt realization transcends individual paths and experiences, reminding us that although diverse in our journeys, we are all interconnected and eternally intertwined.

As we engage in the necessary inner work, cultivating conscious awareness and expanding upon our consciousness, we unlock dormant potential encoded within our DNA, tapping into the vast reservoir of knowledge and wisdom that lives within us. With love as the guiding force, we liberate our DNA, allowing it to receive new energetic signatures that are infused with the highest frequencies of technology. This journey toward unlocking our DNA and expanding our consciousness is a deeply personal one. It requires us to delve into the depths of our being, to confront and clear any energetic blocks or limiting beliefs that hinder our growth. Through this inner work, we gain access to new levels of awareness and understanding, allowing us to tap into the infinite potential that is already inside us. As we become consciously aware of our thoughts, words, and actions, we begin to align ourselves with the highest expressions of love and compassion. This alignment fosters a deep sense of interconnectedness as we recognize that each individual is on their own unique path, facing their own challenges and lessons. In this state of unity, we move beyond judgments and expectations and accept others as they are, offering love and support without condition, but with boundaries in order to protect ourselves.

The journey toward enlightenment is a lifelong process, one that requires dedication, self-reflection, and a commitment to growth. It is not a linear path but rather a continuous spiral of evolution that we shed old patterns and beliefs, and then, finally, step into our truest and highest selves. The tools for this transformation are already included within our DNA, waiting to be unlocked and activated. Meditation, intention setting, energy healing practices, de-programming, and self-care rituals are just a few of the examples of the tools that we have to support us on the journey.

In embracing the power of our words, we recognize that they hold immense creative potential. Our words serve as spells, casting intentions into the universe and shaping our reality. By consciously choosing our words and speaking from a place of love, abundance, truth, and empowerment, we align ourselves with the frequencies of creation and manifestation. Each step on this journey is a conscious choice to embrace our true nature, to become the highest expression of ourselves. We see beyond the illusion of separation, and recognize the interconnectedness of all beings and all things. We understand that love is the guiding force, and by embodying this love we can contribute to the collective evolution of humanity. The path to enlightenment is supposed to have obstacles; nothing is given freely, as we have to do the work to get there. It requires courage, perseverance, and a willingness to confront our shadow aspects. Yet, as we continue to do the work, shedding layers of conditioning and limitation, we move closer to our true essence and the realization of our highest potential.

Taking a balanced and objective perspective to examine my experience, it is worth exploring the power of the mind. If one does not acknowledge the existence of extraterrestrials, then the possibility arises that all these extraordinary experiences were created by the mind itself. It opens up the idea that, through the power of the mind, I could have potentially healed myself. If indeed everything unfolded through the power of my own mind, then it suggests that anyone has the ability to dive into their own mind, heal themselves from their suffering, and become the catalyst for their own personal and collective evolution.

The power of the mind is intricately intertwined with the principles of the universal laws that govern the fabric of existence. One of these fundamental laws is the law of attraction, which suggests that like attracts like. The thoughts and beliefs that we hold in our minds emit vibrational frequencies that resonate with corresponding experiences and outcomes in the external world. In other words, what we focus our minds on we attract into our lives. Where your attention goes, your energy flows.

The power of the mind also aligns with the law of cause and effect. Our thoughts and emotions are like subtle energies that ripple out into the universe, eventually returning to us in the form of circumstances and events. The mind becomes the causal force that initiates a chain reaction, creating a ripple effect of consequences in our lives and our surroundings. The power of the mind can be seen in relation to the principles of the law of mentalism as well. The law of mentalism suggests that all is the mind, and that the universe is created through mental manufacturing. This implies that the external reality we experience is ultimately a projection of our internal thoughts, beliefs, and perceptions. By consciously redirecting our thoughts and shaping our mental landscape, we become active participants in co-creating our reality. The power of the mind also aligns with the principles of faith and intention. The minds unwavering faith and conviction in the fulfillment of our desires can activate the forces of the universe to work in our favor. Setting clear intentions and infusing them with positive emotions directs our minds toward the manifestation of those intentions, opening doors to extraordinary possibilities. In essence, the power of the mind operates within the framework of universal laws, interweaving with the energetic fabric of the cosmos. By understanding and harnessing these laws, we can actively participate in shaping our reality, manifesting our desires, and unlocking the boundless potential that resides within our minds.

I have zero doubt that my experience was genuine, so I don't rely on the power of the mind in this way for any belief. In truth, the power of the mind is how I manifested this experience in my reality.

Below are questions to contemplate when exploring the topic of extraterrestrial contact and your alignment with it.

- Are my beliefs and preconceptions about extraterrestrial contact influenced by fear or judgment and, if so, how do these emotions impact my openness to such experiences?

- Am I limiting my own potential for connection with extraterrestrial beings by holding onto societal fears and preconceived notions about what such contact may entail?

- Do I find myself judging others who share their extraterrestrial contact experiences, and if so, how does this judgment affect my ability to remain open-minded and empathetic toward their perspectives?

- What expectations do I hold regarding extraterrestrial encounters, and how do these expectations influence the way I interpret and engage with reports of such experiences by others?

- Have I explored any unconscious biases or conditioning that might be hindering my receptivity to the possibility of extraterrestrial communication or visitation?

- How can I cultivate a sense of curiosity and openness to different interpretations of extraterrestrial contact experiences without imposing my own beliefs or expectations on others?

- Do I feel a sense of resonance or alignment with the concepts of extraterrestrial contact, and if not what internal barriers or doubts may be contributing to this disconnect?

- Have I taken the time to reflect on my own fears or uncertainty surrounding the idea of extraterrestrial beings and their interactions with humanity?

- How can I shift from a place of fear or skepticism toward the space of curiosity, acceptance, and exploration when it comes to the possibility of extraterrestrial contact?

- In what ways can I deepen my understanding of extraterrestrial phenomena and engage in conversations with others who have had experiences with an open heart and mind, free from judgment and preconceived notions?

CHAPTER 9:
Researching Contact through Mediation—What I Found

From the moment I woke up the morning after my contact, a heightened sense of consciousness engulfed me, not only regarding my experience but also in relation to my entire life. My brain was buzzing with activity. I immediately felt a strong urge to share my story, regardless of what others might think, because it was my undeniable reality. I have never before had a dream where I remembered every single thought with such clarity. Every sentence, every detail, it all made perfect sense and aligned exactly with what had transpired before I even went to sleep. I experienced emotions, thoughts, and a complete recollection of the entire event.

Nothing about it felt like a dream. While I acknowledge that some people may interpret it differently since it occurred during the night, I had never before encountered a dream where I could recall every thought, interaction, emotion, and word exchanged. This profound experience left me in a state of hyper awareness. Suddenly I became acutely aware of all the issues I have been struggling with, no longer desiring to engage in them. Everything that had caused me suffering, everything I asked help and guidance for, had vanished. No dream had ever manifested itself in real life before like this had. I began living my life in a completely different way, passionately seeking out others who had similar experiences. I started to research contact through meditation and watched every documentary available on extraterrestrial encounters. Eventually I stumbled upon someone who was conducting contact experiences through meditation in group settings. This resonated with me deeply because of my own experience, and how it unfolded organically, without any prior guidance. While most people report visual sightings of UFOs or drones in the night sky, I couldn't actually find anyone who had encountered extraterrestrials in person like I had. As fate would have it, there was an expedition scheduled to take place very close to where I live, exactly one year after my initial contact experience. To me, this was a sign filled with serendipity and alignment, true Divine Timing.

That week in Tucson was one of the most impactful in my life. I had no idea what awaited me there. It seems to be a pattern in my life that I encounter both incredible blessings and challenges simultaneously. Once again, the ebb and flow of energy remained consistent in my karmic journey. My experience was a mix of the best and worst moments, tightly woven together into a beautiful package. On my very first day, I found myself among a group of nearly thirty individuals. Everyone gathered in a circle, and we shared our reasons for being there. I was third from the last of the entire circle to speak. As I spoke about my experiences, I felt validated when the leader of the group recognized that my heart was the focal point of my experience, something they also say is relevant to make contact.

After the conversation, we took a break for lunch and planned to engage in remote viewing upon our return. This would be my first attempt at remote viewing. Each of us had our own unique motivations for participating. While some sought out personal-contact experience of any kind, the primary focus of these expeditions was to retreat into the desert, observe the night sky, and document any peculiar or unexplained UFO phenomenon. Capturing content during these expeditions held significant importance for them. The discussion preceding our attempt at remote viewing centered around its historical context. It was the first time I learned about individuals who had gained fame in the past through their proficiency in this practice. It appeared that these individuals had close association with psychic abilities and that the government had utilized them for various experimental purposes. Before we got into the remote viewing exercise, we were instructed to engage in thirty minutes of meditation, connecting with our higher selves. We were asked to inquire about what the group facilitator had put in a box earlier that morning.

As the following thirty minutes unfolded in silence, my mind raced with excitement about being present in this moment and the exhilaration of just being there, getting to share my own story. I found myself focused on my sense of elation during the meditation. I did manage to attain a state of being fully present, which is a state of being connected to my higher self naturally. When the allotted time passed, the facilitator proceeded to go around the circle, asking individuals what they had visualized about the contents in the box. Again, I was the third from last of the participants, and up until that point, no one had provided an accurate answer. When it was my turn, I felt a sudden surge of urgency. I closed my eyes and requested guidance from my higher self about the contents of the box. In my mind's eye, I received a vivid image of a sparkly circle, reminiscent of a shimmering diamond, but distinctively perfectly round. Instinctively, I pondered what a sparkling circle could represent, and the words *crystal sphere* resonated inside of me. I said, "Crystal sphere," and the facilitator of the group looked at me with surprised curiosity, prompting them to inquire about the color. Again, I shut my eyes and glimpsed shades of glittery pink, leading me to describe it as pinkish.

To everyone's (including my own) astonishment, the facilitator revealed a rose quartz crystal sphere in the box, confirming my accurate perception of a pink crystal sphere. This was another testament to my profound bond with stone, my heart, and my higher self.

I cannot adequately express my elation in that moment. It was a profound satisfaction, as I had wholeheartedly trusted and validated my connection to my higher self in front of an entire group of strangers. It was my first time trying remote viewing as well! I would dive even deeper into my connection with my higher self after this experience, and I discussed some details of those deeper personal meditations in a previous chapter.

Regrettably, the energy that countered my earlier favorable experience came in the form of disbelief. As we embarked on our nighttime expedition into the desert, I noticed a peculiar hostility and anger directed toward me whenever I asked questions or made any statements. I was always engaging and inquisitive, and this is a part of my authentic nature, typically something I've always been praised for. I couldn't fathom where this rude energy was stemming from. The group was divided into carloads for convenience, and I happened to be the driver of a larger vehicle that could accommodate all of the necessary supplies. This meant that my group consisted of four individuals, including myself, plus our supplies. Once we arrived at our remote desert destination, we were essentially confined until the entire group decided to leave. During one of our breaks, I made a few comments that were met with an unexpectedly hostile response from the facilitator. I had mentioned a physicist that I read about, who had discussed the concept of a unified consciousness theory. Instead of engaging in a thoughtful conversation, I was belittled in front of the entire group for discussing someone else. I naïvely explained that I was merely highlighting the empowering aspects of this physicist's unified theory of consciousness, and wondered how it aligned with our own evolution. To my surprise, they approached me, and said I was a small person for discussing people and that big people discuss ideas, even though that is what I thought I was doing. Their hostile accusations left me feeling small and deeply hurt. Nonetheless, I made an effort not to let this altercation overshadow the rest of my trip. However, it seemed as though they had turned their back on me and proceeded to test my resolve. The group of people riding in my car all recognized the hostile atmosphere, and were perplexed by the sudden tension.

That evening, feeling unsettled, I turned to the Internet to investigate the possible reasons behind the animosity between the two individuals involved. A quick search revealed several interviews featuring both of them. It became apparent that, somewhere along the way, the facilitator and the physicist had experienced a falling out, and the facilitator seemed to be taking out their frustrations on me. Adding to the misunderstanding, I had mispronounced the physicist's name due to my limited familiarity with their work. The facilitator, however, considered me a suspicious figure and treated me like a spy. Initially, I contemplated leaving the trip altogether due to the treatment I received. However, another member of the group convinced me to be the bigger person and stay. Reluctantly, I made the decision to continue, although I refrained from making comments or actively engaging, despite that being my natural inclination. The following day, another individual from the group approached me during our break, offering an apology for the facilitator's behavior, and provided insight into how their demeanor had been shaped by their personal experiences over the years. It became apparent that nearly half of the group members were loyal to this leader, each discreetly monitoring the rest of us from the separate car groups. This revealed a deep-rooted insecurity and mistrust within the group's leadership. The prevalence of unbalanced masculine energy in their approach was evident. Most individuals have only known an unbalanced masculine energy perspective in life, because that's the energy that has been available to us. As someone with a connection to the feminine and with profound insights on the topic being preached, I realized that there was much they could learn, possibly even from me. My presence there seemed to serve as an opportunity to offer a different perspective on energy, allowing for a shift away from the dominance of unbalanced masculine energy in their interactions and meetings.

Toward the end of the trip, the facilitator seemed to ease up on me slightly, and even offered somewhat of an apology for their earlier harshness. They went on to explain their belief that everyone is constantly spying on them, given the nature of their work involving meditations for contacting with extraterrestrial beings, despite them not actually having had any personal-contact experiences themselves, only recordings of strange movements of lights in the night sky.

During our nighttime desert expeditions in Tucson, the purpose of me being on this trip became evident as I absorbed hours of their extensive lectures during that week. The facilitator appeared fixated on their own quote about light eradicating darkness. I attempted to initiate a discussion regarding the concept of darkness, expressing that energy as a whole does not possess inherent good or evil aspects. There isn't a distinct good or evil side of energy, only varying levels of heaviness and lightness. These aspects are in a constant state of balance and movement. There exists a long-standing history of depicting the darkness, the feminine mother energy as representing evil. Demonizing the mother is done because lower-frequency vibrationally charged humans want to blame something instead of having accountability for their unfavorable deeds and actions. Blame keeps humans in the victim state of mind, and does not contribute to the evolution of human consciousness. In truth, our existence is not dualistic, where opposing forces perpetually conflict with each other. Rather, it is a world of polarity, where everything strives for equilibrium and balance. There are two sides to every energetic frequency and then there is balance. Neither light nor darkness inherently possesses good or evil attributes; instead, they can lead to favorable or unfavorable circumstances. According to the universal laws that we know of, energy is in a constant state of motion and continuously seeks to achieve equilibrium. These laws also acknowledge the interconnectedness and unity that exists at various levels, reflecting the concept of as above, so below. Within this framework, it is recognized that both favorable and unfavorable aspects exist across the spectrum of energy. What may be beneficial or good for certain individuals or situations may not necessarily be beneficial for everyone or everything, and vice versa.

The facilitator frequently expressed their deep affection for these expeditions, where they would venture into the heart of nature and establish a connection with the land in remote locations. This active engagement with grounding negative energy is considered a very healthy thing to do for any balanced lifestyle. Negative grounding energy (aka, dark mother energy) exhibits certain aspects that may be considered heavy, but should not be equated with evil. The concept of darkness, in this context, carries equal relevance and plays a crucial role in maintaining balance. While it may not always showcase the same qualities as light energy, it holds its own significance within the larger framework of existence.

Whenever I seek understanding on the interplay between darkness and light, I simply retreat to my garden. Each day in this sanctuary reveals a tapestry of contrast between darkness and light that resonates deeply within me, perhaps because of my affinity for the mother. Amidst the growth of my blackberries, I observe a metaphor unfold—the intertwining thorny vines, the dance of sunlight upon the berries, and the delicate balance between light and the dark shade. As the berries flourish in the desert heat, those kissed by direct sunlight bear scars of over-exposure, while hidden beneath the leaves in the dark live pristine, sun-protected gems. Be cautious, though, because those thorns are vicious if you want to eat those berries! So, in order to nourish your body with those berries, you may have to endure some pain along the way. This natural spectacle reminds me of the importance of equilibrium: the need to seek shelter at times, to preserve our essence and sweetness, just as the berry thrives in the shade to avoid being scorched from too much light. Painful moments in our lives often lead to catalysts for growth, just like the blackberry teaches you to navigate the thorns to nourish your body. Like the berry, we too rely on the interplay of light and darkness for sustenance and growth. Without light we wither, and with too much we burn out. It is in this delicate balance, mirroring the dance of the garden, that we find balance and harmony.

Consider any plant as an example. It thrives and grows with the help of light, but its stability and nourishment come from having its roots firmly established in the darkness. In the darkness, decomposed decayed matter—death—becomes nutrients that support life at the plant's roots. If the plant is exposed to excessive unbalanced sunlight, it may wither. However, the darkness retains the information about the plant, holding the codes for its return to life with stable roots once it gets what it needs to balance itself. Dark energy derived from the earth transforms everything into substances that we utilize in the light. Darkness in our lives fosters true alchemy. Light does not exist without darkness, just as darkness is incomplete without light, as it is within the realm of light that all living entities express themselves. The darkness holds all the codes for life to express itself. It is the most perfect expression of balance, and of life in the cosmic dance. Polarity in energy entails the existence of opposite and contrasting elements within the energetic spectrum. It is the interplay between these polar forces that generates balance, harmony, and growth in the universe. Positive and negative, light and dark, Yin and Yang—these polarities are fundamental aspects of energy. They coexist and interact, each influencing the other, in a perpetual dance of dynamic equilibrium. Polarity adds complexity to the fabric of existence, thereby fostering diversity and the continuous flow of energy. It is through the contrast between polarities that we gain a deeper understanding and appreciation of the myriad expressions of energy. Whether it's the ebb and flow of life's rhythms or the fusion of opposing forces, polarity is an essential and intricate aspect of the tapestry of the universe, shaping the very essence of our existence.

Even our human bodies are naturally designed to sleep in the darkness and be awake in the light. During graveyard shifts, people may alter their natural circadian rhythms to work at night and sleep during the day. Yet, even when we sleep, our eyes are closed in darkness, allowing our brains to reset and find balance. Scientific studies on rats show that they will die after a period of eleven to thirty-two days without sleep. There are ethical limitations for research on humans, obviously. Sleep-deprivation studies show a decline in cognitive abilities, hallucinations, and severe impairments physically, as well as an increased risk of chronic conditions, which highlights that we cannot solely thrive in the light; we need darkness to achieve balance. Another example of polarities is life and death, which we can further break down into light consciousness and our dark, earthly bodies. The consciousness associated with the masculine, father energy represents light, while our bodies stem from the dark, nurtured by Mother Earth. Our light consciousness will manifest in another body and animate it. Death is not an end; it is a new beginning, as it must exist this way to sustain new life. This is the eternal, perfect system. What often frightens us, leading to the creation of a perception of evil, is how death appears—leaving behind the body, skeleton, and unpleasantness once animation fades. This is why internal work is essential, to learn that the soul endures and will live on in a different space to learn new lessons. We are inherently perfect and just need to remember our origins. In the vastness of space, as our perfected evolved selves, it is sterile and the only way to continue to grow is to begin again. We get to experience life again and spread our genetics. The creation of spiral galaxies that can support life and evolve in polarity is truly remarkable. What we often call evil are actually the actions of humans. Many humans do indeed act upon their sick states of mental health, which is also another reason we need to promote evolved consciousness. Once we raise the vibrations of humans, then the planet will also undergo an uplifting to a higher frequency. This does not mean that darkness will be eradicated; this means that the acts of humans will be less than they were—less harmful, not gone. There will be a period of peace, and then unbalanced feminine will create new issues we need to evolve through, then peace again. It is cyclical and never-ending, until the earth is no longer a good habitat for humanity.

Another illustration of polarity can be found in our current existence on planet Earth. We have designated the poles at the end of the Earth as North and South, which continuously maintain a state of equilibrium. The North and South Poles of Earth serve as vital anchors, maintaining equilibrium as our planet spins and journeys through space. The dynamic magnetic forces at the poles differ significantly, contributing to the planet's rotation and gravitational balance, which enables life to thrive and dance gracefully through the cosmos. It is not accurate to label the North Pole as inherently positive or negative, or to assign such classifications to the South Pole either. Nor can we categorize one as good and the other as evil, as this is the intrinsic nature of all things—an interplay of energy, movement, and balance. As above, so below.

Polarity is a fundamental aspect of our existence. Polarity over duality encourages us to see the full spectrum and embrace both sides. This dance is symbiotic to our existence. The idea of good and evil should be untangled from that of right and wrong. Determining what is right or wrong is a deeply individual experience, and each person possesses a unique energetic signature shaped by their planetary alignments, parental influence, karmic soul journey, and various other factors. As a result, the definition of right and wrong is inherently personal and varies from one individual to another, with degrees of similarities. Religions that originated from the desire to govern through fear have prevailed for millennia, reflecting the dominance of unbalanced masculine Yang energy. This form of energy seeks power and control, employing any means to achieve it. However, in our contemporary era, these antiquated paradigms no longer resonate with our human experience. People are increasingly awakening to the realization that fear-based manipulation has long dictated their lives, sparking a revolution of their mind. The evolution of consciousness commences when we consciously engage with our surroundings, habits, and conduct. Acknowledging the manipulation and deceit perpetuated by others for the sake of power and money prompts the initiation of our transformation.

The ongoing shift in consciousness can lead us to realize that the societal framework constructed around us was designed to confine us, distorting our self-worth and promoting consumerism over self-enlightenment. Every industry thrives on making you feel inadequate, perpetuating self-doubt and competition to fuel economic growth. By sowing division and fostering rivalry among people, humanity's unity is compromised, hindering a quick and seamless social transformation. So, it remains crucial for humanity to aid in breaking the mental shackles that constrain us. To shatter our preconceptions and unravel the fabric of our existence, we must engage in deep introspection to unearth our true purpose.

It is our heart that enables us to reach deeper levels of awareness, particularly when we seize opportunities that foster a connection between our logical mind and the resonance of our heart. This communion allows us to transcend logical understanding and tap into deeper emotional insights. By integrating the rational with the intuitive, we can navigate our experiences with a fuller perspective, leading to greater clarity and purpose in our lives. I think we can all agree that humans need to improve emotional intelligence, which starts in the heart.

Exploring the concepts of polarity versus duality, good versus evil, or letting go of any preconceived ideas requires deep introspection. The following questions will help you with that that self-examination.

- How can I differentiate between polarity (the inherent contrast and balance of energies) and duality (the perception of fighting within separation) in my own life and beliefs?

- In what ways can I transcend the societal construct of good and evil to embrace the understanding that all energies exist to offer balance and contrast for growth and evolution?

- How can I release preconceived notions and judgments about individuals expressing different energies, recognizing that their actions stem from conditioning and experiences unique to their own journey?

- Have I considered that individuals who exhibit behaviors considered to be evil may have been shaped by unfavorable experiences and mental health challenges, leading them to react in ways they were conditioned to respond?

- How can I shift from blaming and condemning others for their actions to understanding that they operate from their own learned perspectives and experiences, contributing to the intricate tapestry of balance and growth in the collective consciousness?

- What role do societal narratives and imprints from history have in shaping our beliefs about good and evil, and how can we transcend these limiting paradigms to foster a more holistic understanding of energies and expressions?

- How does the recognition of masculine and feminine qualities in individuals contribute to a deeper appreciation of the diverse expressions of energy without assigning blame or judgment?

- In what ways can we identify the interconnectedness and influence of energies, understanding that each expression serves a purpose in the grand tapestry of existence?

- How can we challenge the narrative of fear and control perpetuated by imbalanced power structures, recognizing the importance of individual sovereignty and discernment in navigating societal influences?

- How can we cultivate a sense of inner balance and harmony between masculine and feminine energies within ourselves, embracing the wholeness and unity of all expressions without falling into the trap of assigning blame or division based on perceived differences in energy manifestation?

CHAPTER 10:
Remote Viewing—From the Heart Portal

Remote viewing is a fascinating psychic phenomenon that involves the ability to gain information about a distant or unseen target via the use of sensory perception (ESP). It is an ability in which individuals can tap into nonlocal information, enabling them to perceive events, locations, or objects that are inaccessible through ordinary perception. Remote viewing gained popularity through the efforts of the U.S. military and intelligence agencies during the Cold War era. It acquired accountability through a research program, known as Project Stargate, which was conducted by the Stanford Research Institute (SRI) and later transferred to the Defense Intelligence Agency in the 1970s. This program aimed to explore the potential military applications of remote viewing and harness the capabilities of individuals who demonstrated this extraordinary psychic skill.

One of the key figures associated with popularizing remote viewing is Ingo Swann, an artist and psychic who became the focal point of research at SRI. Swann's exceptional ability in remote viewing astonished researchers, and provided significant evidence for the notability of this phenomenon. His work laid the foundation for the development of protocols and training methodologies that are still used today. Aided by the guidance of researchers like Harold Puthoff and Russell Targ, Swann's remote viewing experiments paved the way for subsequent investigations into the psychic skill. The successes of Project Stargate included accurate remote viewing of specific targets, which attracted both skepticism and intrigue from the scientific community and the general public.

Despite its controversial nature, remote viewing has continued to be explored and utilized in various forms to this day. After the closure of Project Stargate in the 1990s, many of the former military remote viewers transitioned into independent research and training organizations. These organizations, such as Farsight Institute and the International Remote Viewing Association, continue to push the boundaries of remote viewing and its potential applications. Within the remote viewing community, protocols have been refined and standardized to improve the reliability of results. These protocols often involve structured methodologies and standardized target templates that help minimize influences and increase the accuracy of remote viewing sessions. Remote viewing techniques have been applied to various domains, ranging from historical and archaeological research to medical diagnoses. In the field of archaeology, remote viewers have provided insights into ancient civilizations, assisting in the discovery and documentation of archaeological sites. In the medical field, remote viewing has been explored as a potential tool for diagnosing medical conditions, complementing conventional diagnostic procedures.

Remote viewing has also found its way into the realm of personal development and spiritual exploration. Individuals interested in further exploring their innate psychic abilities and connecting with their higher selves often engage in remote viewing training programs and workshops. These endeavors cultivate and harness the inherent intuitive and psychic potential within all individuals. While remote viewing continues to intrigue us, it is important to note that it remains a subject of scientific debate. Skeptics argue that the lack of consistent results cast doubt on the validity of remote viewing. However, proponents of remote viewing points to numerous successful demonstrations and experiments as evidence of its potential and importance. The diverse outcomes observed in remote viewing can be attributed directly to the connection of the individual conducting the psychic exploration. Given that not everyone reaches the same depth of self-awareness, the results vary accordingly. Psychic abilities can stem from various senses; some rely more on intuition and feeling, while others manifest through touch or auditory perceptions. As a result, each individual's unique psychic ability contributes to the varying results seen in remote viewing experiments.

Remote viewing from the Heart Portal is an interesting approach to the practice of remote viewing that emphasizes the use of the heart's intuitive intelligence and gathering information about distant or unseen targets. This technique recognizes the profound connection between the heart and intuitive perception, integrating both logical analysis and emotional resonance. Traditional remote viewing primarily focuses on mental processes, such as visualization and analytical thinking. However, remote viewing from the Heart Portal takes into account the wisdom and intelligence that resides within the heart. The heart is considered a gateway to higher consciousness, providing access to intuitive insights that go beyond the limitations of the logical mind by shifting the focus to the heart. The goal is to tap into a more holistic and compassionate perspective. It involves cultivating a state of heart coherence, which is a harmonious and synchronized rhythm between the heart and the brain. This coherent state enhances the intuitive capacities and facilitates access to non-local information. Remote viewing from the Heart Portal recognizes the importance of emotional intelligence and empathic resonance. It acknowledges that emotions carry valuable information and can serve as a guide and compass in the remote viewing process. This approach encourages remote viewers to attune themselves to the energies and emotions associated with the target, allowing them to gather a deeper level of understanding and connection.

Incorporating the heart into remote viewing can enhance the quality of information gathered during a session. The heart possesses an innate sensitivity to subtle energetic cues, enabling remote viewers to access not only visual information but also the emotional and energetic vibrations of the target. This expanded perception leads to a more comprehensive understanding of the target, transcending mere visual descriptions. Remote viewing from the Heart Portal also promotes a sense of interconnectedness and compassion in the remote viewing process. As remote viewers tap into the heart's intelligence, they develop a deeper sense of empathy and connection with the target. This connection allows for a more profound and compassionate engagement, fostering a greater appreciation for the unity and interconnectedness of all existence.

Practicing remote viewing from the Heart Portal requires cultivating heart coherence through techniques such as heart-focused breathing, gratitude, and intentional shifts in emotional states. These practices facilitate alignment with the heart's wisdom and open the door to intuitive insights. While remote viewing from the Heart Portal may not be widely recognized or embraced within traditional remote viewing circles, it offers a unique and transformative approach to the practice. It recognizes the power of the heart's intuitive intelligence and its ability to access information beyond the constraints of analytical thinking. By embracing the heart as a portal for remote viewing, individuals can tap into a profound source of wisdom and connection, enriching their remote viewing experiences, and their heart's resonance, as well as themselves.

We are energetic electrical beings. We give, receive, transform, and transmit energy, and our hearts generate an electromagnetic field that extends several feet beyond our bodies due to the electrical pulses produced when the heart beats. These electrical signals are strong enough to create a measurable electromagnetic field, detectable with sensitive instruments like magnetometers. The heart and brain communicate through electrical impulses, and the coherence between these two organs creates a harmonious field that positively impacts our well-being. Destructive emotions such as anger and anxiety can lead to chaotic and distorted fields. However, when we cultivate a harmonious state characterized by beneficial emotions, including love, gratitude, and compassion, we generate a coherent field.

The heart also houses a complex network of neurons known as the heart-brain, consisting of approximately 40,000 neurons. These neurons play a role in regulating heart rate, rhythm, and responses to various psychological and emotional states. The heart-brain interacts with the central nervous system, sending and receiving signals that influence both cardiac function and our overall state of health. This interaction is essential for effectively managing our emotions and stress, ultimately impacting our heart health.

Now that I have gained a foundational understanding of remote viewing and heart coherence, backed with experiences from using both of these processes, I can confidently affirm that not only is contact with our highest selves achievable, but contact with inter-dimensional beings is also possible though our heart portal. These beings are benevolent in nature and can only interact with humans in ways that aid their evolution and our collective growth. During my contact experience, my heart opened up the dimension that allowed contact to be made. My higher self was my voice, and it came from a place of pure love, which was my soul's consciousness—detached from any personal gain, embodying the greater-good mentality.

Some people call this space the fifth dimension. It is just another aspect to existence we have to tap into, a layer that can be unveiled after we strip away the false ideologies and masks. These inter-dimensional beings are here for our collective good and evolution. Their presence and interactions are guided by wisdom, love, and complete respect for the interconnectedness of life. When we approach them from a heart-centered space that is rooted in selflessness and the desire for the greater good, we align with their intentions and create a harmonious bridge of communication.

Moving forward, my intention is to integrate more heart coherence in my meditations, and into my present work. By cultivating heart coherence, we not only enhance our individual connection with our higher selves but also create a frequency of love and harmony; that vibration ripples out into the collective consciousness. This intention aligns with the path of unity and oneness, inviting a more compassionate, loving, and evolved earth experience. As we deepen our understanding of these practices, we recognize the complex system of interconnectedness within all realms of existence. By cultivating heart coherence and aligning our intentions, we embark on this journey of expanding consciousness with love and a commitment to the evolution of both ourselves and our world.

Challenges of remote viewing within a group setting can arise when not everyone holds the same level of trust or understanding of the phenomenon, as well as lacking the same level of trust in themselves. It can lead to skepticism and doubts, particularly when one individual demonstrates accuracy in remote viewing skills while others may not have experienced the same success. In such instances, it is important to remember that remote viewing is a highly subjective experience, influenced by each individual's level of intuition, receptivity, and psychic abilities. Just as not everyone possesses the same musical or artistic talents, not everyone may have an aptitude for remote viewing.

These differences in abilities and experiences can create skepticism or disbelief among those who may not fully comprehend or relate to the extraordinary nature of remote viewing. To address this challenge, it is crucial to maintain open and respectful communication within the group. Sharing personal experiences, insights, and findings can help foster understanding and create an environment of trust and acceptance. Providing explanations about the process of remote viewing, its scientific background, and its historical usage in various domains can also help to expel misconceptions and doubts. It might be beneficial to encourage others in the group to explore their own intuitive abilities through training and practice sessions. This can offer them an opportunity to personally experience the potential of remote viewing and gain a deeper understanding of its validity before engaging in it during group settings.

Ultimately, it is important to maintain confidence in one's own ability and experiences, even in the face of skepticism. Reflecting on your own journey and personal insight, achieving accurate results can build self-assurance and serve as a reminder that remote viewing is a genuine phenomenon that exists beyond any prejudices. Rather than seeking validation from others, focus on personal growth and continued exploration of one's own intuitive abilities. In any given scenario, consistent practice leads to improved performance. Having a balanced state of heart coherence is crucial, and an individual's capability to utilize psychic abilities depends on their specific circumstances.

While I may have successfully performed remote viewing on my first attempt, it was not my first interaction with my higher self. I have cultivated a profound and enduring connection with my higher self over a significant period of time. Plus, my planets are already aligned, thereby having intuitive and empathic tendencies naturally, making remote viewing something innate within me.

Toward the conclusion of my experience in the desert of Tuscon, I came to realize that group coherence plays a large role in facilitating better contact experiences. Although I had some reservations about how I had been treated earlier in the week, I continued to reach out to my higher self, asking her to reach out to the Beings to make their presence known. I wanted to understand their perspective on the situation and the circumstances I found myself in. I knew that they were aware of my presence. During one of the group meditations in the desert, I sensed their presence observing us from beyond our circle, yet they did not reveal themselves to the group, only to me. However, during the expedition on the final night they did make their presence unmistakably known by positioning their massive ship directly above us. The group facilitator opened up to us, expressing apologies on the last day, and everyone seemed to be in better spirits.

During the last night's expedition meditation, I felt an intensely dense and heavy energy descend upon me, which I instantly recognized as a spaceship. As soon as I felt this happen, the facilitator exclaimed, "There's a ship right on top of us!" and I concurred. This harmonious energy and coherence could have been established throughout the entire experience, except that distrust hindered it. Now I understand how crucial it is for everyone to be aligned and on the same page for the energy to flow as it should, allowing any occurrences to manifest without being hindered. In every experience there is a lesson, and every person is a teacher. I was taught many lessons on my trip, but I also got to teach during this experience. Having an empowered, enriching way of navigating our lives helps to facilitate more of these types of experiences in it.

Here are a few questions to assist in assessing heart coherence in your human experience.

- How often do you consciously engage in practices that promote heart coherence and emotional equilibrium in your daily life?

- When faced with challenging situations, do you notice a difference in your emotional and mental clarity when your heart is in a coherent state?

- In what ways do you believe heart coherence impacts your interactions and relationships with others?

- Have you observed any connection between achieving heart coherence and your overall sense of well-being and resilience?

- How does heart coherence influence your ability to navigate stressful or demanding circumstances in your personal and professional life?

- How can you deepen your understanding of heart coherence and the heart portal to enhance your remote viewing capabilities and tap into your innate intuitive wisdom?

- Have you noticed a correlation between practicing heart coherence and accessing heightened states of awareness or expanding consciousness during remote viewing sessions?

- What steps can you take to cultivate a harmonious connection between your heart's intelligence and your intuitive faculties to facilitate clearer and more profound remote viewing experiences?

- In what ways can you prepare yourself holistically, mentally, emotionally, and spiritually to fully embody your inherent remote viewing abilities through heart coherence and intention?

- How do you envision integrating the principles of heart coherence, the heart portal, and remote viewing into your daily life to unlock your innate potential and navigate multi-dimensional aspects of reality with clarity and purpose?

CHAPTER 11:
Making It Your Own— Navigating Your Authentic Path

By now, you possess the necessary tools to navigate the depths of your own heart, navigating your human experience. All you have to do is seek guidance by calling upon your higher self for assistance.

It is crucial that you choreograph the dance of your life—your energetic dance of light. Design a map, prepare your course, and steer yourself in the direction of your truest desires. Take a moment and honestly assess how your attention is focused and where your energy is flowing. Cultivate endless patience and unconditional self-approval, stepping back to gain a broader perspective of the whole picture. When you connect with the vastness of all that is, you come to realize that you are inseparable from the whole. This awareness is the key to abundance, as abundance in all aspects resides within the whole. Giving is the dynamic energetic counterpart of receiving. Just as the universe dances and sings throughout the cosmos— sending, receiving, and respecting the laws of energy in creation—so to can you participate in this harmonious exchange. Sound, a sacred tool, played a vital role in our evolution and remains an invaluable resource. It is the most potent tool at your disposal, freely accessible from within you. Sound is in abundance and accessible at all times. Sound is a frequency code.

When you tap into the nurturing energy of the mother, you gain a deeper appreciation for all that she does to sustain your physical body, allowing it to bask and grow in the light. In return, all she asks is for your body back, which she helped cultivate, to continue nurturing growth and expansion in its own unique and transformed way. Retreat, recharge, and reassess. Soil requires nourishment to fuel plant growth, so too must you nourish what allows you to grow and evolve. The mother's lesson of stillness and silence nurtures the inner self and prepares you to shine your brightest when the time is right.

Remember you are a part of everything, intricately connected to the whole. Remember the moon waxes and wanes, capable of retreating or shining as needed. Remember that you are a part of the sun, a part of all the planets, whose energies have been imprinted upon you at birth. Remember that your consciousness came here like a laser beam; you are a light soul, here to create, expand, and evolve conscious awareness into that of knowing your true self. You came here from a higher consciousness, and you've been given all the tools that remain inside your DNA to unlock your true potential. The answers you seek are already present, woven into the lessons and teachings that surround you. When you calm your mind, your physical being, and your environment, you can tap into the wisdom and knowledge you seek. Embrace the understanding that making mistakes is a natural part of the learning process. The shadow side does not wish to be forgotten; it simply craves presence and acknowledgment. Even as we strive for growth and evolution, we still remain human.

Every successful individual will attest to the plethora of mistakes and failures encountered along the path to success. Growth necessitates an environment that challenges us, and the stressors are pivotal to our expansion. Anyone claiming a perfect life as a human is unlikely to experience any real growth, as true growth is generated from learning from our mistakes or hard times. Perfection is an illusion on this earthly plane. The only aspect approaching perfection is the portal of your heart, which operates from a different perspective: a selfless and altruistic perspective.

The heart portal serves as a navigational compass through your mistakes, providing the strength to overcome obstacles. When you operate from the heart, you discover true motivation, rooted in heartfelt intentions. It is through these intentions, grounded in love and aligned with the universe, that you create your own unique experiences and find your authentic path. By attuning to your intentions, driven by passion and empowered by love, you will discover true success, a transcendent experience that elevates your consciousness to new levels. Success in love means desiring the best outcomes, not only for yourself but also for others. The heart portal imitates a state of abundance, and by aligning with that state, feelings of abundance permeate your life. As you feel abundance, desires actually diminish, creating space for deeper connections with the essence of your being, and the unified whole.

Jiddu Krishnamurti intelligently remarked, "It is no measure of one's health to be well adjusted to a profoundly sick society." When we observe the system that governs our lives, it becomes glaringly apparent that it is fundamentally flawed. Those entrusted with the responsibility of providing assistance and care often perpetuate the same societal patterns and operate within the confines of this hyper-capitalist framework. However, there are individuals who are challenging the status quo and transforming the way they approach their work, aiming for different outcomes. While they may not have all the answers on how to fix the system, those who are willing to try are driven by a purpose beyond monetary gain.

As humans, it is imperative that we constantly strive for growth, expansion, and improvement. To truly become better versions of ourselves, we must embrace change. The current societal structure is threatened with inequality, suffering, and injustice. In order for us to evolve as a species, we must actively engage in practices and actions that foster progress and equality. It begs the question: What harm would come from promoting a certain quality of life for all of humanity?

The pursuit of a better world built on principles of fairness, compassion, and collective well-being requires a paradigm shift. It necessitates a departure from the individualistic, profit-driven mindset that currently dominates our society. We must dismantle the barriers that perpetuate inequality and establish systems that emphasize the value of human life over material gain. This fundamental restructuring allows for a more holistic and inclusive approach, one that places the well-being of all individuals at the forefront. Imagine a world where access to quality healthcare, education, and basic necessities is not determined by one's wealth or social standing, a world in which compassion, empathy, and cooperation prevail over greed.

By prioritizing the welfare of our fellow human beings, we create an environment in which every individual is afforded the opportunity to thrive and contributes to the greater good. What if every individual was provided a fulfilling life that satisfied their basic needs, granting each person the freedom to choose their own path? Even though individual outcomes would still be influenced by personal effort, starting from an equal footing for all seems to make more sense. By offering equal opportunities to everyone, individuals can determine their own potential rather than having societal norms dictate their capabilities. Addressing fundamental human needs such as sustenance, shelter, and security on a collective scale serves as a foundational solution that can uplift society as a whole. When these essentials are guaranteed, those inclined to excel can thrive, while those seeking comfort and peace find the peace that they desire, and those with artistic aspirations can pursue their passions. Innovators contributing to humanity's progress, such as inventors of clean perpetual energy, should absolutely receive abundant rewards for their valuable contributions. When humanity's basic needs are met, true luxury is already achieved.

The global scenario today mirrors historical disparities like master and slave dynamics, but with different terminology. The prevailing struggle for dominance and power is persuasive, but we are transitioning toward a more enlightened awareness that harmonizes with nature's teachings.

Critics may argue that such a vision is unrealistic or unattainable, but it is through our collective efforts and a commitment to change that we can overcome the limitations of our current society. We must challenge the conventional notions of success and redefine progress in terms of genuine human flourishing. It requires us to break free from the confines of a profit-centric mentality and redefine our values as a global community.

Progressive individuals and groups have already begun taking steps in this direction. They are working tirelessly to address social, economic, and environmental issues, advocating for systematic change, and promoting inclusivity. Their multi-faceted approach encompasses a range of efforts, including policy reform, grassroots activism, community initiatives, and conscious consumerism. This broad spectrum of actions reflects a shared commitment to building a more just and caring society.

Ultimately, the transformation of our society begins with a shift in consciousness, a collective awakening to the inherent interconnectedness in all beings and our responsibility to one another. It is through the shared understanding that we can collectively redefine our social systems, paving the way for a more equitable and harmonious existence. In our pursuit of a better world, let us not be resigned to the complacency of a sick society. Instead, let us embrace the challenge, united in our determination to effect positive change. Together, we can create a society that nurtures the well-being of all individuals and upholds the values of compassion, justice, and equality.

Staying on course implies that you are navigating your life. In today's fast-paced world, it can be challenging to stay focused and on track with our goals and aspirations. Distractions are everywhere, vying for our attention and preventing us from making progress. However, there is a powerful tool that can help us combat these distractions and maintain our focus: boundaries. By establishing boundaries for ourselves, we can effectively deal with life challenges and eliminate unnecessary distractions. Keep in mind that boundaries are not meant to restrict us but rather to empower us on our journey toward personal growth and success.

It is important to understand their various meanings and purposes. Boundaries are often created due to a lack of something within ourselves. We should never blame others for triggering us. If we find ourselves triggered by taking things personally, engaging in damaging self-talk, adopting a victim mentality, or resorting to blame, it is our own internal issue that requires setting a boundary. Taking responsibility for our healing journey is crucial, as boundaries are meant to serve us without being used against others. The need for boundaries does not stem from the fault of another person; it is our own responsibility to heal. To achieve healing, we must not internalize what others say, and we must realize that their words reflect their own inner state. A healed individual comprehends the range of emotions and energies that can influence others, avoiding the need to assign blame for sporadic occurrences.

It is crucial to understand that boundaries are for us and us alone. They are not meant to control or limit others, but to safeguard our own well-being and productivity. By defining clear boundaries, we assert our right to prioritize our own needs and goals, establishing a healthy and balanced approach to life. To create effective boundaries, it is essential to identify our strengths, weaknesses, and priorities. Self-reflection is key to understanding what truly matters to us and what areas of our lives are prone to distractions. By recognizing our limitations and areas of vulnerabilities, we can strategically set boundaries that address these specific concerns. For example, if we struggle with procrastination, we can establish a boundary of dedicated work hours, free from any non-essential distractions.

Once we have identified our boundaries, it is vital to communicate them with others. Articulating our boundaries reinforces our commitment to ourselves and informs others of our expectations. It is important to remember that setting boundaries is not about confrontation but rather about healthy self-assertion. Clearly and respectfully communicating our boundaries allows others to understand our needs and to respect our personal space and time. In addition to communicating our boundaries, it is equally important to consistently reinforce them. This requires discipline and self-awareness. It may be helpful to create physical and mental signals that remind both us and others of these boundaries. For instance, we can establish a designated workspace to signal our dedication to focused work or set reminders on our devices to limit our daily social media usage.

By consistently upholding our boundaries, we create a habit of self-discipline and increase our ability to stay on course. Another valuable aspect of establishing boundaries is learning to say no when necessary. Sometimes we may feel obligated to take on additional responsibilities or commitments that hinder our progress. However, by setting limits and knowing our own capacity, we can confidently decline opportunities that do not align with our goals or strain our resources. Saying no is not a selfish act, but rather an act of self-preservation and self-respect. It allows us to prioritize our time and energy and focus on what truly matters.

It is necessary to review and reassess our boundaries periodically. As our circumstances and priorities evolve, our boundaries may need adjustment. Life is dynamic, and what worked for us in the past may not be the most effective strategy in the future—or the present. By regularly evaluating our boundaries, we ensure that they remain relevant and aligned with our current needs and aspirations.

Boundaries can help us break free from the mentality of people pleasing. People pleasing can have a significant adverse effect on our well-being. This behavior often attracts those who seek to feed off of your energy, as well as individuals who may want to take advantage of you. When you firmly establish your boundaries, you shift your focus from pleasing others to pleasing yourself. This isn't about being selfish; rather, people pleasing is a behavior developed within society, heavily influenced by capitalism, that encourages us to cater to others' wants and needs. As a result, we often dilute our true selves to gain approval. Adopting an empowered way of authentic living teaches others that it is okay not to conform to every-one's expectations and needs, promoting a healthier mindset within soci-ety. When we prioritize our own needs and desires over others', we attract authentic relationships with people who respect our boundaries.

Being a people pleaser typically stems from a desire for attention, which doesn't always benefit us. This behavior can signal a lack of self-con-fidence, boundaries, and self-love. Once we cultivate our authentic qual-ities, the need for people pleasing diminishes. Being assertive is not the same as being aggressive; assertive individuals simply express their needs confidently. In a world dominated by a hyper-capitalistic system, many fall into the trap of people pleasing. However, our true essence is in fulfilling our self through authentic means, rather than seeking empty validation from others. By focusing on our own fulfillment, we can foster healthier, more genuine connections.

Navigating the heart involves a journey of authentic self-expression, cultivating compassion, and deep self-exploration. It entails listening to your intuition, building trust within yourself, and embracing daily mind-fulness practices to empower your decision making, aligned with your purpose and true self. This form of navigation extends into meditation, allowing creative exploration in neural pathways. This new way of navigat-ing our minds is spurred by evolving conscious awareness. Navigating the heart involves prioritizing care for each other, our planet, and ourselves. Loving ourselves is essential, as genuine love for others comes from self-love. This self-love transcends the need for external validation, freeing us from people pleasing, unhealthy relationships, or seeking conditional love. Embracing self-love enables us to recognize our capacity for compassion and understanding, acknowledging that we are all capable of errors, foster-ing a forgiving and compassionate attitude toward all.

Self-love serves as the cornerstone for establishing heart coherence, as it enables individuals to embrace their true essence with sympathy and acceptance. When one nurtures a deep sense of love and appreciation for oneself, it paves the way for inner harmony and coherence with the heart, leading to a profound alignment of body, mind, and spirit. This genuine self-love acts as a catalyst for fostering the state of coherence where emotions, thoughts, and actions are in sync, creating a powerful resonance that radiates love both inwardly and outwardly.

Heart coherence is significantly enhanced when you express yourself creatively and authentically in various ways. This heightened state of heart coherence not only amplifies conscious awareness, it also supports a deeper sense of alignment with yourself and with the world around you. By engaging in authentic expression, you unlock a pathway to aligning your thoughts, emotions, and actions, promoting an unfathomable understanding of self and an increased sensitivity to the interconnectedness of all things. This practice cultivates a greater sense of presence, allowing you to tap into your inner wisdom with a heightened level of clarity and purpose.

Reflect on the following questions to increase your sense of presence.

- What are my spending habits? Do they support like-minded individuals with a greater-good mentality?

- Are my purchasing decisions aligned with my values and ethical beliefs? Am I supporting companies that prioritize sustainability and social responsibility?

- Do I research the brands I buy from to ensure that they align with my ethical standards? Am I mindful of the impact of my purchases on the environment and communities?

- What are my current habits and viewpoints on reusing, reducing, and recycling, and how do they reflect my values? What steps can I take to improve the environmental impact in my daily life?

- Do I take responsibility for my choices and not blame external factors for my own shortcomings? In what ways do I hold myself accountable for my actions and decisions?

- How can I cultivate empathy and compassion in my daily life to positively influence those around me? In what way can I align my heart's desires with actions that contribute to the greater good in my community?

- Am I aware of any tendencies to shift blame onto others or external circumstances? How do I actively work on taking ownership of mistakes and shortcomings?

- What limiting beliefs or fears are hindering me from following my heart and making a meaningful impact? How can I balance my personal needs with the responsibility I feel toward making a difference in the world?

- What steps am I taking to increase my self-awareness and conscious awareness in everyday life? In what ways am I consciously educating myself and growing to make more intentional choices?

- Have I forgiven myself and others, recognizing that everything serves to help me become a better person? Have I embraced forgiveness on all levels?

CHAPTER 12:
What Comes Next—Putting it all Together

Writing this was probably my most difficult chapter, because it reflects my real life—my plans and aspirations for the future. For me it feels like journaling as I navigate through my thoughts and feelings, still figuring it all out. I don't have a specific area of focus; rather I'm driven by my desire to help others who may be on a similar path. I aim to embody the change I wish to see in the world. Raising my son has always been my primary goal, but now that he is an adult, it's time for me to explore the next stage of my life. I feel fortunate to have had the opportunity to continue my education over the past seventeen years while being a mother. This journey has enriched me with various skills, enabling me to assist others effectively as I carve out my own path moving forward. Now, I'm eager to apply what I've learned and have a meaningful impact.

Embracing the present moment is the key to living in your light, yet we recognize that the world often presents challenges that make it difficult to maintain that state of being. Perfection is not the goal; rather the focus is on growth and evolution. Moving forward, it is crucial to create an environment where individuals are recognized and appreciated for their vulnerability and courage in authentically living according to their own truth rather than conforming to societal expectations. This is the next crucial step. While many have discussed these ideas, it is important to take action. What are you personally doing to contribute to the greater good? Are you following the patterns of others, or are you approaching life from a holistic perspective, a humane vantage point, and a mindset that prioritizes everyone's best interests? It is through concrete actions, aligned with the benefit of all principles, that we collectively move forward and create definite change. I am reminded of a heartfelt lesson my son taught me when he was only four years old.

I am predominately right-handed, but I can also be ambidextrous. However, my son is left handed, but also has the ability to be ambidextrous. I used to playfully refer to him as the "backwards man," because he would do everything in a mirrored or backward way. Whether it was his left-handedness or his spelling, he would do things in a reverse manner. I had observed this trait in my father, who was left-handed and wrote backward as well. I would try to show my son something, but he would never mimic me. Instead, he would do it his own distinctive way. One time I found myself frustrated, asking him to simply do exactly as I did. In response he looked at me, rolled his eyes, and said, "Mom, if you can do it like that, then of coarse I can do it like that. I just want to do it my own way." He then confidently grabbed the crayon, put it in his right hand, and accomplished the task exactly as I had asked—making sure I understood that he could do it like me. He was just more interested in exploring his own unique approach. In that moment, I began to grasp—on a small scale—what he meant. I realized that I needed to stop pressuring him to imitate me, and instead allow his creativity and abilities to flourish in whichever direction he showed interest. Since he began his teenage years, I have witnessed him teach himself to play four different musical instruments. He approaches each instrument in a different way, because he already sees how it is conventionally played. He simply wants to be original and express his own uniqueness, which is a characteristic associated with Aquarians. He has seven astrological energetic expressions in the fourth house of Aquarius, which is why I call him my Aquarian Portal Master. His talent for channeling innovative ideas and exploring his creativity while thinking outside the box aligns perfectly with the Aquarian Age. My son will forever remain one of my greatest teachers, reminding me to embrace individuality and the power of self-expression.

These are the qualities we should embrace as we move forward: the willingness to try new approaches and depart from broken systems. Do we truly need to mindlessly repeat everything we are shown and are told? Must we simply mimic one another? Perhaps the genius displayed by my son at the age of four is precisely what we need. The Era of Aquarius is believed to usher in an eon marked by intense changes in consciousness and human behavior. It is said to bring forth a heightened sense of individuality, innovation, and humanitarianism, as well as a greater emphasis on collective collaboration and spiritual growth. Some anticipate that this energetic shift will prompt people to embrace unconventional ideas, seek truth and meaning, and strive for societal progress and harmony. I perceive these changes already manifesting. It is becoming increasingly evident that we must clear the path and make room for something new, something better.

We are compelled to discard the old to construct a fresh future from a different vantage point, as the current energy presents unique opportunities. This metamorphic energy is already palpable and noticeable in our daily experiences. Rather than discarding the past, let us leverage it as a foundation for realizing our potential to create something better. We can identify the aspects that are effective and focus on enhancing those traits. By integrating his-story and discovering the truth within it, we can transform it into our-story. Her-story is our-story, because mother holds the keys and codes, and they have always been there for us to uncover.

Achieving enlightenment is a lifelong journey that involves learning complex life lessons along the way. As spiritual beings having physical bodies on this dynamic and polarized planet, our consciousness continues to evolve. We will keep returning until we successfully achieve our goals and learn to live in harmony with our planet, until we can no longer utilize its resources. During a meditation after my extraterrestrial contact experience, I sought guidance about the future of humanity. The answer they revealed to me was that I already possess the knowledge, that I am already attuned to the cycles of the universe. It reminded me to tap into my higher self for answers. When I did, a surge of energy and information flooded my being, illuminating everything with crystal clarity.

Our solar system exists within an arm of the spiral Milky Way galaxy, and when we look out into the cosmos we see countless other spiral galaxies, among other creations. This reinforces the Universal Law of Correspondence, as above, so below, demonstrating that the creation systems we encounter here on earth are mirrored throughout the cosmos. Our understanding and awareness are still in infancy, but we continue to explore our consciousness and have much to look forward to. Our planet's past reveals cycles of evolution and cataclysmic events. Dinosaurs dominated the Earth for hundreds of millions of years, during the Triassic, Jurassic, and Cretaceous Periods. Each hundred million years showing an evolution of the dinosaurs and the planet. Each period last hundreds of millions of years, and then a meteor wiped them out. However, the dinosaurs did not return. All life flourished once again, while we emerged on our evolutionary journey. This serves as a reminder of the potential for future meteor-based disruptions. Evidence of such events exists, such as the mile-wide crater in Arizona and the impact crater off the coast of the Yucatan, which is believed to be the result of the meteor that caused the last dinosaurs' ultimate demise.

By observing nature, we can easily distinguish the differences between the eastern and western hemispheres. It becomes apparent that the evolution of various species thrived predominately in the eastern hemisphere, while the western hemisphere experienced a significant decline. Naturally, large land animals were exclusive to the eastern hemisphere. The distinction suggests that the location of the impact following catastrophic events played a crucial role. The closer a location was to the strike location, the more severe the consequences for animal and plant life. As a result, the eastern hemisphere, with its longer history of evolution, boasts remarkable diversity of animal and plant species. This includes magnificent creatures such as the great apes, elephants, giraffes, and hippos, among others. The growing awareness of these cosmic phenomenal events might explain humanity's fascination with reaching Mars and seeking to establish a presence beyond our planet. Perhaps this arises from a desire for greater control over our own evolutionarily journey. Our awareness of potential asteroid impacts has prompted significant investments and programs aimed at deflecting these celestial threats. However, can we recognize that these impacts do not necessarily result in the destruction of our planet? Rather, they serve as a resetting mechanism. The Earth and its natural balancing act have experienced five major ice ages throughout its 4.5 billion-year history, demonstrating an ability to preserve itself by maintaining equilibrium. These fluctuations are supported by scientific evidence and emphasize the enduring cycles of the earth's existence. In the event of a cataclysmic occurrence on earth, the potential heating of the atmosphere to extreme levels might necessitate the planet's self-balancing act through an ice age, acting as a means to prevent widespread death. Evidence of this phenomenon is observed in the remains of animals, frozen with green food in their mouths, indicating an instantaneous freeze brought on by an ice storm. So we see the system we inhabit is inherently perfect, although it may not always align with our preferences or lead to favorable outcomes during challenging times.

This system persists because our perception of time is interconnected with the gravitational forces at play within it. Life as we know it is structured by the existence of this system, specifically designed with gravity. In space, however, evolution takes on a different form, devoid of the bodily rhythms that result from the interaction between organisms and the sun, time, and gravity. The diverse nature of existence across different environments highlights the intricacies and variations within the universe. As we observe nature, we recognize the inevitability of change and the importance of embracing the present moment. Each individual's path to their best life is unique, highlighting the significance of avoiding judgment or comparison with others. While the laws of nature remain constant, the energetic imprints shaping each person's experience are diverse and distinct within this dynamic framework.

The future holds inevitable transformations for subsequent generations, with the likelihood of facing challenges, such as another ice age. Just as a woman undergoes cycles of change in her life, the planet experiences her own shifts, including the ebb and flow of energies leading to events like an ice age. Our past cultural narratives often reflect similarities in origin stories, hinting at the possibility of preserving advanced consciousness for future cycles or safeguarding individuals with heightened awareness. In the face of potential cataclysmic events, there is a looming uncertainty that could disrupt communication channels and alter the course of human interaction as we know it today. Adaptability and resilience in the face of unpredictable changes become vital components of preparing for an uncertain future. Given the uncertainty of the future and the fleeting nature of the present moment, it is prudent to nurture human compassion proactively, rather than waiting for circumstances to compel us toward it.

Preparing ourselves for a scenario where some may harbor feelings of superiority or entitlement requires laying the foundation of compassion and unity now, in order to mitigate conflicts and discord in the future. Relying on money as a solution proves futile in times of crisis, as its value diminishes when faced with fundamental challenges. True evolution lies in cultivating compassion and unity preemptively, fostering a heightened state of consciousness and interconnectedness within society. Prioritizing the well-being of farmers, who are particularly dedicated to sustainable practices that preserve the planet, is paramount. Supporting those who uphold environmental stewardship ensures their readiness to assist in times of need. The unpredictability of what lies ahead necessitates the shift toward educating ourselves and future generations on sustainable living practices, moving away from unsustainable practices. Through collective efforts to prioritize compassion, unity, and environmental consciousness, we can build a resilient foundation for whatever changes may come our way, fostering a more sustainable and harmonious future for all.

Understanding the future of humanity can be challenging for those deeply entrenched in the current offerings of the world. A broader view of humankind recognizes that change is an unavoidable aspect of our reality. The inevitability of change is a constant in our existence, as nothing remains static or unchanged. This perpetual evolution prompts us to reflect on why some individuals, including ourselves, may resist change. Fear of stepping out of our comfort zones often hinders acceptance of change, limiting our exploration of the diverse opportunities the world presents.

As we expand our awareness through scientific and quantum discoveries, our perception of time and existence evolves. This growth opens doors to a deeper understanding of our cosmic origins, including the concept of reincarnation. Reincarnation serves as a process for continuous learning and species development, guiding us toward higher realms of intelligence and consciousness. Despite the perceived complexities of the system, there's a sense of intrigue and joy in revisiting experiences and evolving through various forms of existence. Imperfection adds depth to our journey, unveiling layers of discovery and growth.

Humanity's role in spiritual altruism should focus on building a supportive community rather than commercializing the essence of spirituality. It is essential to create a network where individuals assist each other based on their needs, without the emphasis on profit. Unfortunately, those who do not pursue excessive desires or material aspirations often lack opportunities and may face challenges such as homelessness or succumb to the pressures of consumerism and capitalism. Exploiting spirituality for financial gain perpetuates an unjust system where access to spiritual growth becomes restricted by economic status. Transforming spirituality into commodities with inflated prices for experiences that should be accessible to all contradicts the essence of spiritual teachings and fairness. The practice of selling spirituality at exorbitant rates only serves to benefit those offering it, disregarding the spiritual journey's true essence and accessibility. True spirituality transcends monetary value and is naturally free for all to embrace. The notion of attaching a price tag to spiritual teachings perpetuates division and inequality based on financial means, deviating from the core principles of unity and inclusivity. In a society driven by hyper-capitalism, it is understandable why some may seek financial gain from spirituality, but this practice ultimately perpetuates societal divides and goes against the fundamental values of spiritual enlightenment and compassion. Let's explore avenues for cultivating a personal spiritual practice, devoid of monetary constraints or external directives, where the focus is on self-guided meditation to uncover insights and wisdom independently.

Remember sound as a free frequency code? That is but one free frequency code—let's explore other various forms of this free frequency phenomena.

Free Frequency Codes

Free frequency codes are aspects of life that are available for us to work on at any time. There is an abundance of resources on these subjects, which can all be found on the Internet, and no money is required to do inner work through meditation.

- Love and compassion: Embrace unconditional love and cultivate deep compassion for yourself and others.

- Gratitude and appreciation: Practice gratitude daily, acknowledging and appreciating the blessings in life.

- Forgiveness and release: Let go of past hurts and grievances, forgiving yourself and others to experience emotional liberation.

- Authenticity and self-expression: Embrace your true essence, expressing yourself authentically without fear or judgment.

- Abundance and prosperity: Align with the frequency of abundance, recognizing and attracting prosperity in all areas of life.

- Healing and balance: Promote physical, emotional, and spiritual healing, restoring balance within yourself and the world around you.

- Unity and oneness: Recognize the interconnectedness of all beings and embrace the frequency of unity and oneness.

- Joy and playfulness: Embrace joy and inner childlike playfulness, infusing your life with lightness and happiness.

- Intuition and inner wisdom: Tune into your inner guidance and trust your intuitive knowing, allowing it to guide your path.

- Expansion and growth: Embrace challenges as opportunities for learning and development.

There are certainly more free frequency codes that we can explore, such as mindfulness and presence, courage and strength. It's essential to listen to our inner self and identify what areas we need to focus on. There is a wealth of information and countless frequency codes available to us to use on our spiritual journey.

There are many free resources available for exploring these free frequency codes that exist within nature and the universe. All you need already exists within you and around you. Please explore more than just these obvious ones I mention here, as the world needs to share free resources with each other now more than ever.

- You: Everything you need to succeed is inside of you right now. It always has been, and it always will be. If a balanced lifestyle is in your life choices, then of course you control your thinking and your words and sounds. Exercise is free. Meditation is free. Chanting is free. Music is free. Mantras, mudras, and meditation are all free. Dancing is free. Pure bliss and joy is free! Your hands create at your will, free of charge from the mind. Your inner wellspring of energy never asks for money. You are pure energetic magic.

- Social media: Platforms like TikTok or Discord have become invaluable free resources for personal healing and growth. Users share their journeys, insights, and coping strategies in engaging videos, while live streams often feature sound healing, meditation, and yoga sessions offered for free. These interactive experiences create supportive community for those seeking comfort and inspiration.

- Insight Timer app and YouTube: These platforms have a wide range of free content, including guided meditations, nature sounds, chanted mantras, spiritual music, or sound healing therapy sessions. There are numerous free videos for Yoga and Pilates classes, and tons of clean-eating videos to help you stay on track.

- Mother Nature, aka Gaia: Embrace the opportunities presented by the great outdoors and venturing to nearby parks, forests, or picturesque areas, allowing yourself to connect with the profound healing frequencies that nature offers. Community gardens are a great way to revitalize your earthly energies, cultivate organic foods, and be a part of community endeavors. While taking extravagant vacations to culturally vibrant destinations might be enticing, it is not a necessity. You have the ability to cultivate the land where you currently reside and tap into the same powerful energy. By investing your own blood, sweat, and tears into nurturing the land, you establish energetic bonds between yourself and the land, ultimately initiating a revitalizing flow of newly shared energetic bonds.

- Chanting and mantra groups and websites: Join local chanting groups or access online mantra resources where you can learn and engage in sacred chanting practices. Consistent repetition is the cornerstone of imprinting information into our minds, enhancing our ability to recall, and ultimately influencing the shaping of our reality.

- Prayer circles or drum circles: Participate in free prayer circles or drum circles, or join online spiritual communities that provide opportunities for collective prayer and guidance. Normally these are free or donation based if you borrow a drum.

- Sound-healing workshops and webinars: Many practitioners host free sound-healing workshops or webinars where you can experience the transformative power of healing sound frequencies and immersions. Sound should always be free!

- Public libraries: Explore the spiritual and meditation sections of your local library. Public libraries provide a wide range of free resources that may include digital media, online databases, educational courses, computer and Internet access, various events and workshops, children's programs, meeting spaces, and space where you can access tons of online resources.

- Podcasts: Podcast platforms host numerous episodes dedicated to meditation, spirituality, sound healing, and other related topics, providing valuable insights and practices.

- Online music platforms: Access free spiritual or meditation playlists on platforms like Spotify, Soundcloud, or Bandcamp, featuring a wide array of calming and transformative music. You can help support local artists in this fashion.

- Community events: Keep an eye out for local events, workshops, or festivals focused on meditation, sound healing, yoga, and spirituality, as they sometimes offer free attendance or introductory sessions.

I would like to acknowledge that some of these resources may involve a small upfront cost, and I understand that they are not entirely free. However, that is why I listed you as the number-one resource, as you don't require anything else except yourself. Other resources such as a phone or Internet service are things we might already have. If you have a vehicle, it can take you to the local library or you can utilize bus passes and ride-sharing options to reach your destinations like prayer and drum circles. The Insight Timer app offers a wide range of free resources that can be accessed once you have a phone. Additionally, local coffee shops often provide free Internet access, with the minimum requirement of purchasing a cup of coffee.

I would like to express that while I hold no opposition to capitalism, it seems that it has become overly dominant, leaving little room for other aspects of life, such as spirituality, to receive due attention. Spirituality and economic matters are inherently distinct, and finding a balance between them can be a delicate endeavor. It is important to acknowledge that living in this world requires financial resources. Therefore, it becomes vital to navigate our spiritual path harmoniously with our financial circumstances. Free spirituality is a basic human right. However, if you find yourself drawn to a class or offering by someone you encountered and it resonates within you, it may be worth it to consider investing in it. Personally, I have spent a significant amount of money on my spiritual journey. I have recognized instances where the primary focus seemed to be solely on monetary gain. There have also been occasions where I found myself exactly where I needed to be, surrounded by beautiful souls who are offering free resources and sharing empowering messages. If you believe you get what you pay for, it is understandable that money holds great significance to you. Nevertheless, by valuing spiritual presence over economy, your priorities align with the inherent abundance that already exists within and around you. It is within that space that you can discover your source of love—love for oneself and for all beings, and love for the process of creation and all its intricate expressions.

I once received insight from a teacher who shared the perspective that money is the agreed-upon energy used as a medium of exchange for various services. While I acknowledge the truth in that statement and do not necessarily disagree with it, my concern is in the classification of spirituality and the pursuit of higher intelligence as a commodity or service. These aspects of life hold a profound and intrinsic value that goes beyond mere transactions and financial considerations. They encompass an innate longing for personal growth, connection, and enlightenment that cannot be reduced to a commodity or measured solely in monetary terms. When spiritual pursuits become accessible only to those who are wealthy, a concerning power dynamic arises where money wields significant influence and control. In such circumstances, there is a risk of prioritizing material wealth over the essential aspects of the spiritual journey.

The essence of spirituality lives in the universality and potential for personal growth and transformation, which should be accessible to all individuals regardless of their financial means. It is crucial to strive for a society where everyone has equal opportunities to explore and develop their spiritual path, fostering a more inclusive and balanced approach to the pursuit of higher knowledge and enlightenment. Money represents the lowest vibrational energy exchange when it comes to spiritual evolution. It is a tree that has been murdered and no longer has a life to feed us food or provide us with oxygen. It is a two-dimensional number on a piece of paper or digital currency and has never even had an energetic vibration. As we strive to access higher consciousness, no monetary value could determine the level of understanding and teaching involved to achieve this. Throughout history, systems were established to exclude individuals so others could hoard knowledge for themselves, maintaining sacred knowledge as a mystery and limiting access only to those who could afford it or who were born into privileged families.

The time has now arrived for us to unveil this mystery to all, enabling the collective to expand its conscious awareness. A mass of energy can catalyze a shift in the paradigm in which we live, as this transformation is already underway. We must either embrace this evolution and adapt to the changing times or fade away with the past. Those who are imparting an empowered way of living, thinking, and being—those who are meant to lead us into the future—are not necessarily the wealthiest individuals, as evidenced by the state of the world today. The manner in which the affluent segregate different classes to maintain power and control reflects that true spirituality cannot be gauged by monetary wealth. Genuine teachers will guide others for the betterment of humanity, as they are in service to humanity. When Yeshua preached his message of light to the masses, he condemned the merchants at the temples, and then went to help the lepers and the prostitutes because they were the ones in greatest need of assistance. This message is the embodied message of light: It matters not where you come from but rather what you do with what you've been given.

With the aim of fostering positive change and having experienced a different lifestyle, my goal is to build something different: A community where mutual upliftment transcends material wealth. Such a community would facilitate support for those in need and create an environment where individuals, regardless of their circumstances, can offer their unique support and gifts. By cultivating a spirit of abundance and sharing, we can raise the vibration of the planet and contribute to a higher collective frequency. By treating each other with kindness and compassion, we can challenge the narratives presented by media and television, allowing us to drive optimistic alterations. Even progress achieved through small steps with occasional setbacks is still progress. Embracing the ebb and flow of life and welcoming diversity strengthens our collective growth. Sharing is caring; whether it is resources, knowledge, or hope, sharing can bring about positive changes and inspire others.

In this pursuit, we have the power to shape the future of humanity. Striving toward progress and evolving as a species requires courage to overcome the control of fear that hinders our advancement. By recognizing this current state of de-evolution in humanity, we can actively transcend the fear mindset and contribute to humanity's growth, ultimately nurturing a brighter, more compassionate, progressive future. My drive stems from a deep well of compassion from personal experiences. The significance of assisting individuals who lack resources is deeply ingrained in my own journey of self-discovery and healing, which was shaped by a lack of resources, guidance, and role models in my life.

I acknowledge that my message may not resonate with everyone, and I fully accept that reality. Realistically, only a small percentage of the population may truly understand the journey toward evolving conscious awareness. While my circle may be modest, I find it fulfilling that even a few are actively committed to expanding their consciousness. I understand that I cannot impose this path on others, only those who genuinely seek self-healing and trust in their own potential will embark on this journey. I'd like to refrain from using words like *believe* as a connotation of effort, because true understanding requires no persuasion; it is simply known and embodied. My role is not to convince but to share my experiences so that others may internalize and apply them to their own growth and healing. Each person's healing journey is unique and not everyone may be ready for it in this lifetime, and that is perfectly acceptable. I respect where individuals are on their path and focus on nurturing authentic connections built on love and understanding.

Moving into this chapter requires considerable courage, as it entails embracing a different path and mindset. For me, what comes next is dedicating myself to inspiring hope and helping individuals achieve the seemingly impossible. Throughout this journey, I strive to assist others in surmounting limitations and unlocking their true potential. If I can overcome my obstacles and achieve personal growth, I firmly trust that anyone can do the same. Despite my progress and growth, I recognize that the ebbs and flow of life remain constant. I do not consistently dwell in my state of light. During moments of meditation, I seek guidance or clarity from my newfound allies. However, these wise companions consistently remind me that the answers I seek are already within me. Through claircognizance, a form of intuitive knowing, I am reminded to tap into my higher self, as she possesses the inherent wisdom and insights that reside with my true essence. In this ongoing journey, I am committed to continually tapping into my higher self, drawing upon her profound intelligence and guidance to navigate the twists and turns of life. It is through this connection that I discover the answers I seek and gain valuable insights into my path forward.

I have recently explored the realm of becoming a death doula through recent courses, only to discover that I had been a light doula all along. I had already completed a course on becoming a light worker, only to realize that I was already one. Being a light worker is essentially the same as being a light doula; it's about guiding others to discover their own inner light. Embarking on the path to becoming a death doula has illuminated my role, not just in the realm of transitioning from life to light but also in recognizing my inherent position of being a light doula, guiding others through the profound transitions of existence. Studying death doula practices aligned well with my knowledge and understanding that death is not the end, rather a transformation; a transition of physical form back to light, on to another form, a continuum of existence. In this awareness, I find a harmonious balance between being a conduit for both light and the transitions of life, embracing the full spectrum of caregiving that involves honoring the journey from life to light and back to life through various forms of existence.

In addition to my journey as a light doula and a death doula, the significance of my connection with the filled twelfth house placements in my natal chart adds another layer to this profound exploration. The twelfth house, known for its association with transformation, beautifully echoes the transitional nature of becoming light, where light serves as the conduit between cycles of existence. This concept emphasizes that we do not permanently embody light; rather it is a mode of transportation during transitions for our consciousness and soul's essence in a continuous evolution of the spirit.

What comes next for humanity is the exploration and cultivation of our intuitive abilities, which we are already witnessing in individuals. These abilities known as clair or *clear* senses—clairvoyance, clairaudience, claircognizance, and clairsentience—serve as our next evolutionary steps toward telepathic communication. To embark on this journey, we must commit to opening up our neural pathways, allowing us to tap into abilities and access the codes the already exist within us. These codes are ingrained in our very being, present within our blood and DNA. We have the potential to communicate with our cellular DNA, enhancing our connection to our true essence plus expansion of our consciousness.

Scientists are exploring expanded DNA and enhanced communication networks that link the brain, the heart, and the gut. These interconnected centers play crucial roles in processing and transmitting information. The brain has 100 billion neurons responsible for conscious awareness. The heart possess forty thousand neurons and has the largest electromagnetic field in the body that send as many messages to the brain as it receives from the brain. Our guts contain approximately 100 million neurons. The brain produces cortisol that regulates our metabolism and blood pressure during stressful times. The gut processes information during sleep and produces 70 to 90 percent of the neurotransmitter serotonin, which is crucial for clear thinking. The vagus nerve is one of the biggest nerves, connecting our gut and our brain. We can see the interconnectedness of these three centers in our body and how they might pertain to the body, mind, and spirit connection, as well as the chakra centers in the body. Unlocking our true potential—to evolve—we must integrate practice of cultivating our conscious awareness into our daily lives, much like practicing personal hygiene. Regular and consistent practice of connecting with our intuitive senses and our body centers will lead to progress, strengthening our abilities and facilitating a deeper understanding of ourselves, the intergalactic world around us, and our creators.

Regrettably, it is unlikely that all eight billion of us will attain enlightenment or reach a consensus on the message I've shared about our evolutionary journey. However, there are significant individuals who already sense the urge to instigate profound changes, capable of ushering humanity into the next phase of its evolutionary path. If a critical mass of us embraces the process, relinquishes fear, and takes the leap into the uncharted territories of surrender without reservation, the potential for us becomes boundless. Our scientific understanding is still relatively limited. Instead of attempting to solve every issue, what if we focused on attaining balance?

The goal could shift from solving all problems to establishing equilibrium, mirroring the balance found in the universe. Exploring science from various angles could assist its advancement. As we progress in our scientific knowledge, we will impact the collective consciousness. Rather than seeking to dominate the planet, humans are meant to nurture and improve the symbiotic connections that already thrive. Valuable lessons can be learned from observing nature; we simply need to shift from a ME to a WE perspective. The word itself is a reflection. A new perspective emerges when we view it from a different vantage point.

When humanity collectively reaches a state of self-actualization and embodies unified consciousness, what we will see is enhanced empathy and compassion for each other. There will be a surge in global cooperation and unity that addresses common challenges, such as poverty and the health care crisis, with us working together for the greater good. You will see enhanced sustainable practices where the focus on sustainability will drive innovative solutions and practices that prioritize the well-being of the planet and future generations. There will be resolution of conflicts that will shift toward peaceful, dialogue-based approaches, with a greater emphasis on understanding and reconciliation. There will be a widespread spiritual awakening and a deeper connection to the universe, fostering a sense of purpose and interconnectedness among us. Individuals will exhibit higher emotional intelligence, leading to more harmonious relationships and effective communication. Society will prioritize the well-being of all its members, promoting mental health, equality, and social justice. Advancements in technology and science will be driven by a collective consciousness that values progress for the betterment of all beings. There will be a celebration of diversity and cultural exchange, promoting mutual respect and appreciation for different traditions and beliefs that are aligned with equality for all. Respecting women during this transitional phase is imperative, since the rising of the feminine energy to counterbalance the overly dominant unbalanced masculine energy is unfolding right now. More individuals will pursue self-actualization, leading to a society where people live authentically and contribute to the betterment of the collective consciousness.

The path to potential contact begins with introspection and the exploration of our connection to our higher selves. By diving inward, we open up the possibility of reaching out to the external realm of our true origins. While this experience may not unfold for everyone, it remains within reach. The presence of information left by our creators serves as undeniable evidence of their existence, signaling the next phase of our evolution. Disregarding their influence means turning a blind eye to the evident signs they have bestowed upon us. Researching deeper to comprehend and establish a connection for contact requires diligent effort on our part. By aligning your intentions with a higher frequency of energy, you can elevate your consciousness to connect with extraterrestrial realms through the guidance of your higher self.

Ascension is like using an energetic vibration as a lasso, connecting it to your desires and pulling yourself toward them. When you link your energy to lower vibrations, it is like descending a ladder. When you link to higher expressions, you elevate yourself to the next level, stepping into a higher realm of consciousness. This process of elevation is what we call ascending. Ascension is the evolution of our consciousness while remaining in our physical bodies. Connecting to higher frequencies means accessing a more elevated energetic state, which translates to improving oneself and situations, fostering more love, and being more connected to the collective whole. By lassoing your intentions into the cosmos, you are sending out a vibrational rope that attaches to what resonates with that energy. If you remain attached to low vibrational networks, you limit your growth and remain in a repetitive cycle. To transcend this and elevate your experience, you must send out a higher vibrational energy through your intentions, thus creating more ropes to pull yourself up to a higher level of consciousness. Ultimately, ascension is about becoming your light by expressing yourself in an elevated fashion.

My upcoming venture involves a community-driven evolutionary social project. I invite you to join me and this community dedicated to mutual support. Community members are encouraged, but not forced, to participate in meditation sessions that will be focused on establishing contact; first within the self and then to inter-dimensional beings. While my website will feature offerings, I plan to conduct regular meetings where I share insights, provide free resources, and discuss various topics involving the ascension of consciousness. These gatherings will serve as opportunities for you to benefit from the knowledge I have acquired, empowering you on your own personal journey of transformation. Rather than divulge all the details here, I prefer to personally introduce you to the initiatives I will be undertaking.

This book serves as an introduction to the exciting new phase along my journey. I anticipate significant changes to unfold as I embark upon this path, aiming to inspire awareness and transformation in others. My focus extends to aiding individuals in initiating the changes they seek in their own lives. While I have devoted considerable time to personal growth, I acknowledge that not everyone is on the same awakening path in this lifetime. Each person's journey unfolds uniquely, and their purpose and significance are intrinsic to their individual light-souls evolution, regardless of their level of consciousness.

In the dawn of our new awareness, may the exploration of humanity's evolution of consciousness help bring about lasting change together, bridging the gap of our separation. Below are questions to consider in the evolution of your consciousness.

- How can you engage in exploration and self-discovery for free in your daily life? What is offered around you that you can utilize?

- In what ways are you actively contributing to the evolution of humanity through your actions and intentions? How are you actively contributing to judgments and comparisons in your daily life that do not contribute to humanity's ascension?

- How are you nurturing your personal growth and evolution on a daily basis? What are your go-to practices for well-being in various areas of your life?

- Are there any valuable free resources or tools that you can recommend to others for their development and expansion? Can you recognize that each person contributing to the betterment of humanity has the potential to unlock the awareness of the collective consciousness?

- What valuable insights or practices have you gained from this book that you are eager to incorporate into your life journey? Will this be something you do alone, or do you want to share with others?

- How can you seamlessly integrate transitions that foster evolution of conscious awareness? What areas of integration will be easiest; what will be the most difficult?

- What are some impactful ways that you can contribute to the collective evolution of consciousness? Have you thought of ways that you are already contributing that aren't mentioned in this book?

- How are you aligning your actions and knowledge to support your own evolutionary growth? Is this something you share with others, or are you afraid of what others might think? Do you judge others for where they are on their own paths? Do you create boundaries out of judgments or are you creating them because you know there is something that you lack?

- Are there any community resources or support networks that you can utilize to enhance your personal and spiritual development?

- How are you preparing for your contact experience?

Namaste and blessed be to those who discover their inner light and courageously follow its illuminating path, regardless of the obstacles they encounter along their journey.

The only difference between the sinner and the saint –
One has realized themselves.
— Sophora Stone

www.SophoraStone.com

Bibliography &
Recommended Reading

Abdullah, Shariff. *Creating a World that Works for All.* Berrett-Koehler. 1999.

Antic, Ivan. *The Physics of Consciousness.* Samkhya Publishing. 2021.

——————. *Samadhi.* Samkhyha Publishing. 2020.

——————. *Metaphysics of Consciousness.* Samkhya Publishing. 2020.

Ashby, Muata. *The Kemetic Tree of Life.* Sema Institute/Cruzian Mystic Books. 2007.

Byrne, Rhonda. *The Secret.* Beyond Worlds Publishing. 2006.

Chaleff, Ira. *Intelligent Disobedience.* MJF Books. 2015.

Clement, Stephanie Jean Ph.D. *Aspect Patterns.* Llewellyn Worldwide. 2007.

Foundation for Inner Peace. *A Course In Miracles.* Foundation for Inner Peace. 2007.

Hanh, Thich Nhat. *The Heart of Buddha's Teachings.* Harmony. 2015.

Howe, Linda. *Discover Your Souls's Path through the Akashic Records.* Hayhouse. 2015.

_____. *How To Read the Akashic Records.* Sounds True. 2009.

Huber, Bruno and Louise Huber and Michael Alexander Huber. *Aspect Pattern Astrology.* Hopewell. 2005.

Jung, Carl. *Man and His Symbols.* Bantam Books Trade. 2023.

_____. *The Undiscovered Self.* Signet Books. 2006.

_____. *The Archetypes and the Collective Unconscious.* Bollingen Foundation. 1959.

_____. *Psychology of the Unconscious.* Digireads Publishing. 2021.

Jupiter Apex of YOD - Jupiter in a Finger of God Astrology Birth Chart. YouTube, HolyCityMystic, uploaded 10, 5, 2023. https://.youtu.be/fcM7phK52x8?si=NBf7txAGWralRYtk.

McKusick, Ellen Day. *Tuning the Human Biofield.* Healing Arts Press. 2014.

Moon Apex YOD-Moon Apex Natal Chart Finger of God Astrology Birthchart. Youtube, Holy City Mystic, uploaded 21, 4, 2023. https://.youtu.be/xCqL8fB8sfE?si=AxR2f7SA2W0C5RGH.

O'Dea, James. *The Conscious Activist.* Watkins. 2014.

Pawluk, William, MD. MSc. And Caitlyn J. Layne. *Power Tools for Health.* Friesen Press. 2017.

Rinpoche, Zap Tulku. *Tara in the Palm of Your Hand.* Windhorse Press. 2013.

Ruiz, Don Miguel. *The Four Agreements.* Amber Allen Publishing. 1997.

Singh, Manhardeep. *12 Laws of the Universe.* Self-published. n.d.

Shoo, Monica, and Barbara Mor. *The Great Cosmic Mother.* Harper and Row. 1987.

Swann, Ingo. *Natural ESP*. Bantam Books. 1987.

_____. *Everybody's Guide to Natural ESP.* Swann-rider Publication, LLC. 2017.

WoolFolk, Joanna Martine. *Scorpio-Sun Sign Series.* Taylor Trade Publishing. 2011.

_____. *The Only Astrology Book You'll Ever Need.* Taylor Trade Publishing. 2006.

Zondag, Karen Hmaker. *The YOD Book.* Samuel Weiser, Inc. 2000.